User Interface and User Experience

Foundational Principles for Interactive Design

Gunikhan Sonowal
Assistant Professor, Faculty of Computer Technology
Assam Down Town University, Guwahati, India

CRC Press
Taylor & Francis Group
Boca Raton London New York

CRC Press is an imprint of the
Taylor & Francis Group, an **informa** business
A SCIENCE PUBLISHERS BOOK

First edition published 2027
by CRC Press
2385 NW Executive Center Drive, Suite 320, Boca Raton FL 33431

and by CRC Press
4 Park Square, Milton Park, Abingdon, Oxon, OX14 4RN

CRC Press is an imprint of Taylor & Francis Group, LLC

Library of Congress Cataloging-in-Publication Data (applied for)

ISBN: 978-1-041-14446-5 (hbk)
ISBN: 978-1-041-20246-2 (pbk)
ISBN: 978-1-003-71576-4 (ebk)

DOI: 10.1201/9781003715764

Typeset in Times New Roman
by Prime Publishing Services

Preface

The book User Interface and User Experience: Foundational Principles for Interactive Design was inspired by a simple observation: despite the rise of digital devices in our daily lives, many continue to be annoying, confused, or blatantly exclusionary. The gap between what designers intend and what users experience is frequently large, and bridging it requires more than technical skill; it also requires a thorough understanding of human psychology, a commitment to inclusive thinking, and a systematic approach to creating experiences that feel intuitive rather than instructional.

The following chapters summarize the fundamental principles that underpin excellent user experience design. They are structured to take readers from foundational thought to practical application, resulting in a complete understanding of how digital products can and should benefit the people who use them.

Chapter 1: Introduction to UI/UX distinguishes between User Interface and User Experience design, tracing their historical evolution from ancient ergonomics to modern digital practices and presenting a ten-step design process that serves as the foundation for all subsequent chapters.

Chapter 2: From Philosophy to Practice lays the groundwork, examining how Human-Centered Design (HCD) serves as the guiding ethical framework, while Design Thinking provides the concrete, iterative method. They work together to create things that are desirable to users, technologically feasible, and commercially viable.

Chapter 3: Psychology of User Behavior examines the cognitive processes that underpin how users perceive, decide, and act. This chapter provides designers with an evidence-based understanding of human cognition, covering Gestalt's laws of visual perception, Hick's Law of decision-making, and the motivational pull of the Zeigarnik Effect.

Chapter 4: Information Architecture investigates the strategic foundation of UX design, namely how content is organized, labeled, and structured to correspond with users' mental models. The four components of IA organizational, labelling, navigation, and search systems are thoroughly examined, as well as the eight principles that drive good structuring.

Chapter 5: Interaction Design examines the communication between people and products using the Five Dimensions framework, which includes words, visual representations, physical objects/space, time, and behavior. Don Norman's basic principles and Nielsen's 10 usability heuristics are useful tools for evaluation.

Chapter 6: Visual Design and Branding explains how aesthetics serve function via scale, hierarchy, balance, and contrast. The fundamental components of visual identity—logos, color palettes, typography, and imagery—are investigated as strategic communication systems that foster trust and recognition.

Chapter 7: Designing for All delves at the relationship between accessibility, usability, and inclusion. This chapter demonstrates how designing for the margins improves experiences for everyone, using WCAG's POUR principles and practical methods.

This book is recommended for those new to UX design, practitioners seeking to deepen their theoretical underpinnings, and anybody interested in the impact of digital encounters on daily life. It does not claim to provide shortcuts or simple formulas; effective design defies reduction to checklists. Instead, it offers thinking frameworks, evaluation principles, and development processes, all of which will be useful long after specific technology has evolved.

The field of UX design entails significant responsibilities. We develop interfaces that facilitate access to information, services, communities, and opportunities. When we design wisely, we eliminate barriers and empower people. When we design irresponsibly, we create more impediments in an already complex world. This book is presented with the intention that its readers will embrace not only the techniques of their craft, but also the ethical significance of their work.

Contents

Chapter 1

Introduction to UI/UX

The design of user interfaces (UI) and user experiences (UX) is a vital field for creating digital products that are both functional and enjoyable for users. UX design considers the entire user journey, ensuring smooth usability, accessibility, and satisfaction. In contrast, UI design focuses on the visual and interactive elements, such as layouts, colors, and typography. The fundamentals of UI/UX design are explored in this introduction, with an emphasis on their distinctions, interconnections, and significance in product development. To align user needs with corporate objectives, a well-executed UI/UX process involves research, prototyping, testing, and iteration. By prioritizing user-centered solutions, visually appealing designs, and intuitive navigation, designers can enhance engagement, reduce friction, and drive product success. Effective UI/UX design, whether for software, mobile apps, or websites, builds bridges between technology and human interaction, ultimately shaping how users perceive and experience digital products. To deliver solutions that are both impactful and easy to use, designers, developers, and stakeholders must possess a fundamental understanding of these principles.

1.1 Definition of UI vs UX

Although UI and UX are sometimes used interchangeably, UI is a distinct subset of UX. According to Figma Designer Advocate Hugo Raymond, "Effective user interface design brings together usability and interactive design to build an emotive connection between users and products" (Hugo Raymond, 2024). An engaging user interface (UI) can therefore significantly enhance the overall user experience of a website or digital product.

DOI: 10.1201/9781003715764-1

The term "User Interface" (UI) refers to the interactive and visual components of a digital product that users engage with. This includes graphical elements such as color palettes, typography, buttons, and icons. The primary goal of UI design is to create an aesthetically pleasing and user-friendly interface that encourages interaction and increases usability.

User Experience (UX) refers to the overall experience a user has while interacting with a digital product. Designing the complete user journey ensures that the product is useful, easy to navigate, and meets the user's needs. UX design encompasses iterative improvements, wireframes, prototyping, usability testing, and user research. Its goal is to deliver a smooth, effective, and enjoyable experience that fulfills the user's objectives and expectations.

The relationship between UI and UX can be compared to a restaurant visit. The UI represents the restaurant's decor, table settings, and menu design, the visual elements that shape first impressions. UX, on the other hand, is the entire dining experience: the comfort of the seating, the attentiveness of the service, the quality of the food, and the seamless flow from ordering to payment. Just as a beautifully decorated restaurant with poor service would disappoint diners, an app with stunning visuals but confusing navigation would frustrate users.

1.1.1 UX vs UI

UX emphasizes the user's engagement and interaction with the product, while UI focuses on its appearance and interface. Together, UI and UX collaborate to create a seamless and successful digital experience. Table 1.1 illustrates the key distinctions between UI and UX design, as outlined by (Mads Soegaard, 2023).

Table 1.1: Key difference between UX vs UI.

Focuses on the holistic experience of the user	Focuses on the specific visual touchpoints of the user
Centers on strategy, structure, and interaction design	Centers on surface-level aspects of design, including visuals
Involves studying the user's journey and designing information architecture	Involves designing the tangible elements of the experience, such as the choice of components and how they interact
Outputs include personas, user journey maps, wireframes, and prototypes	Outputs include mockups, high-fidelity layouts, and prototypes
Incorporates the user's environment, mood, and context	Is more tangible, as users directly interact with the interface

Table 1.1 demonstrates that UX and UI design share similarities in focus and scope. UX (User Experience) design emphasizes the user's overall interaction with a product, encompassing strategy, structure, and interaction design. It involves analyzing the user's journey, developing information architecture, and considering the user's environment, mood, and context. Typical UX design outputs include personas, user journey maps, wireframes, and prototypes, all aimed at creating a seamless and engaging experience.

In contrast, UI (User Interface) design focuses on specific visual touchpoints and surface-level design elements such as visuals, colors, and typography. It entails designing tangible aspects of the experience, including buttons and icons, and their interactions. Common UI design outputs include mockups, high-fidelity layouts, and prototypes, which provide the visual foundation for direct user engagement. Whereas UX addresses the overall feel and functionality of the product, UI focuses on its appearance and interactive elements.

1.1.2 Example of UX vs UI

The distinction between UX and UI is outlined in Table 1.1. To further illustrate this difference, consider the example of a mobile banking app.

The UX design of the mobile banking software ensures that users can complete tasks quickly and enjoyably. For instance, a UX designer might map out the user's journey from logging in to transferring money or checking account balances. Before developing wireframes that define the structure and functionality of the application, they would conduct user research to identify pain points. UX designers may also use personas and user journey maps to demonstrate how different users interact with the software. To detect and resolve usability issues, they would test prototypes on real users, ensuring the app is user-friendly and meets requirements.

The UI design of the mobile banking focuses on the interactive features and visual elements that users can see and touch. To create a consistent and aesthetically pleasing appearance, the UI designer might select fonts, iconography, and color schemes. They would also arrange screens to facilitate the discovery and operation of buttons, menus, and other interactive elements. Interactive prototypes and high-fidelity mockups would be produced to show how each component responds to user actions like button clicks and screen swipes. By designing an interface that is both aesthetically appealing and easy to use, the aim is to enhance the overall user experience.

In summary, the UI designer emphasizes the app's visual appeal and interactivity, while the UX designer ensures its functionality and usability. Together, they collaborate to deliver a seamless and engaging mobile banking app.

1.2 A Brief History and Evolution of UI and UX Design

Although the differences between UX and UI are demonstrated in the preceding chapter, the two have been closely connected to concepts and products from ancient times to the present. This section explores the context of use and the history of UI and UX. A brief overview of their evolution is presented below:

According to Uddin, N. (2023), there is a connection between Feng Shui philosophy and user experience. Feng Shui seeks to harmonize individuals with their environments, much like UX design strives to optimize digital experiences for usability, functionality, and enjoyment. Both disciplines aim to enhance people's lives through innovative design solutions, requiring a deep understanding of human behavior. EMILY STEVENS (2021) categorizes the timelines of UX/UI design, as illustrated in Figure 1.1.

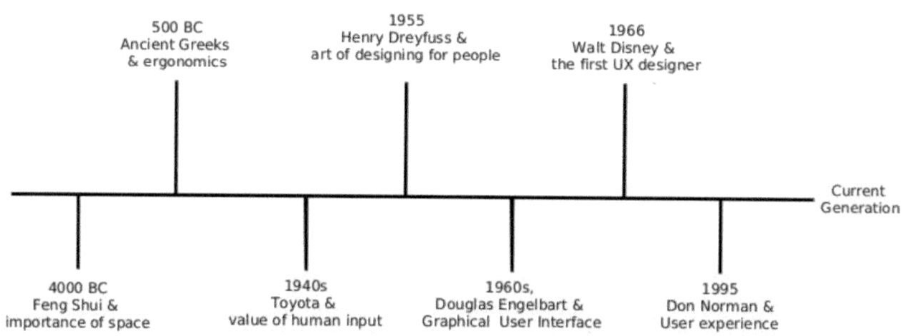

Figure 1.1: History of UI/UX design.

1.2.1 *4000 BC: Feng Shui and the Importance of Space*

Feng Shui is an ancient philosophy and practice that seeks to create harmonious, supportive, and nurturing environments. At its core lies the principle of balance. Practitioners of Feng Shui harness the complementary energies of Yin and Yang to establish harmony within spaces. These energies are expressed through the Wu Xing, or the five elements: water, wood, fire, earth, and metal.

One of the most widely applied aspects of Feng Shui is its theory concerning bedrooms. It provides guidance on arranging elements such as beds, tables, chairs, and mirrors to optimize energy flow. The bedroom holds particular significance in Feng Shui, as it is considered the most important room in a home, where individuals spend a substantial amount of time and find relaxation. As sleep induces a passive state, the energy within the bedroom is believed to have a profound impact on one's overall well-being and mental state.

1.2.2 500 BC: The Ancient Greeks and Ergonomics

Ancient Greece was renowned for using highly developed methods in philosophy, mathematics, and architecture, making it one of the most advanced societies of its era. Greek achievements in religion, art, culture, and medicine had a profound impact on later civilizations, particularly the Romans, while philosophers, such as Socrates and Plato, established the groundwork for Western philosophy.

Innovations including the water mill, water clock, hydria, and Archimedes' screw exemplify the ingenuity of the Greeks and their lasting impact on global development. Early instances of user experience design can be traced to these accomplishments, especially through their understanding of ergonomics in the fifth century BCE.

A notable case is Hippocrates, who described in his writings the ideal arrangement for surgeons. Much like contemporary UX principles that aim to improve usability and efficiency, he emphasized the importance of positioning tools so they were easily accessible and did not obstruct the surgeon's work.

1.2.3 Early 1900s: Frederick Winslow Taylor and the Quest for Workplace Efficiency

According to Taylor's scientific management theory, managers were responsible for creating the most efficient production systems to increase company productivity. In The Principles of Scientific Management, F.W. Taylor (1911) argued that improved management practices could be applied scientifically to address problems in specific labor processes. He believed that the key to raising productivity was optimizing work performance.

A notable example of his theory in practice occurred when workers developed a more effective method for loading pig iron into rail cars using biomechanical research and a stopwatch. As a result, the amount of pig iron almost doubled on the very first day of applying this strategy. Modern UX design reflects a similar principle, aiming to improve business conversion rates by creating better user experiences.

Although the terms "scientific management" and "Taylorism" are sometimes used interchangeably, it is more accurate to view Taylorism as the original manifestation of scientific management. Taylor's methods for increasing efficiency continue to be applied today in companies, the military, and even professional sports.

1.2.4 1940s: Toyota and the Value of Human Input

"The Toyota Way" is renowned worldwide for its effective management of production systems, workers, consumers, and society at large. Toyota's commitment to operational excellence forms the foundation of its success. This excellence extends beyond the tools and techniques for quality improvement that Toyota pioneered in the manufacturing sector.

The Toyota Production System first emerged in the early post-World War II era, a time marked by economic instability and shortages of financial, natural, and human resources. Its primary objective has been to increase production efficiency by continuously and thoroughly eliminating waste, a process that, in today's digital context, resembles decluttering.

The concept was initially introduced by Toyoda Kiichiro, former president of Toyota. Between 1948 and 1975, Ohno Taiichi and Eiji Toyoda refined and advanced the system. Similar to Henry Ford's earlier innovations, the Toyota Production System proved highly effective, but with a more consumer-focused and market-driven approach to product development and delivery.

5S Methodology was developed and refined collectively by Toyota's leadership and engineers, primarily Taiichi Ohno and Shigeo Shingo, as a foundational component of the world-renowned Toyota Production System (Wojtynek et al., 2018). It is a structured approach to workplace organization derived from five Japanese terms: Seiri (Sort), Seiton (Set in Order), Seiso (Shine), Seiketsu (Standardize), and Shitsuke (Sustain), as shown in Figure 1.2. This method enhances operational efficiency by systematically organizing the work area. It involves sorting through all items, logically arranging the necessary ones, thoroughly cleaning, establishing standardized procedures for maintenance, and ensuring these practices are sustained over the long term. Success is driven by team dialogue, which fosters collective agreement on the most effective ways to perform tasks.

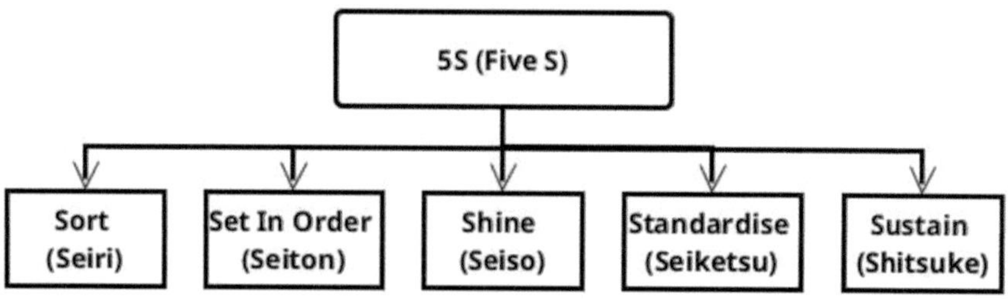

Figure 1.2: 5S (Five S) method.

1.2.5 1955: Henry Dreyfuss and the Art of Designing for People

The first person who comes to mind when discussing usability enhancement is Henry Dreyfuss, best known for his quote, "Designing for people." Dreyfuss, an American industrial designer, created several iconic products, with logic and scientific principles forming the foundation of his design philosophy. In his book Designing for People, Dreyfuss (1959) summarized UX design by stating, "*When the point of contact between the product and the people becomes a source of friction, then the industrial designer has failed*". Conversely, the designer has succeeded if the product makes customers feel safer, more comfortable, more inclined to purchase, more productive, or simply happier. Although his designs are widely recognized, their significance to both historical and modern life is often overlooked. Notable examples include desktop phones, the Hoover vacuum cleaner, and Royal typewriters, particularly the business deluxe model.

Dreyfuss's example serves as a guide for UX designers who should clearly define the time and resources required for user research before beginning a project. If a client does not understand the importance of user research, they should reconsider its value or move on to the next task.

1.2.6 1960: Douglas Engelbart and Mouse-driven Cursor

The oN-Line System (NLS) was developed in the 1960s by Douglas Engelbart as part of his Augmentation of Human Intellect project at the Augmentation Research Centre at SRI International in Menlo Park, California. This computer featured multiple windows for working with hypertext and a mouse-driven cursor. One of Engelbart's primary inspirations was Vannevar Bush's 1945 proposal for the memex, a desk-based information computer.

Engelbart's pioneering work paved the way for innovations at Xerox PARC. In the early 1970s, several researchers moved from SRI to Xerox PARC, where the Alto personal computer was created in 1973. The Alto was the first to employ the desktop metaphor and graphical user interface (GUI), and it included a bitmapped screen. Although never released as a commercial product, thousands of Alto units were built and widely used at PARC, other Xerox facilities, and various universities. By the late 1970s and early 1980s, the Alto had a profound influence on the design of personal computers, inspiring systems such as the Three Rivers PERQ, the Apple Lisa and Macintosh, and the first Sun workstations.

1.2.7 1966: Walt Disney—The First UX Designer

Walt Disney never had the title of UX designer, yet he is often regarded as one of the first. A true visionary, he recognized how advanced technology could improve people's lives. Driven by his passion for creating immersive, authentic, and seamless experiences, Disney World was born (Dickerson, J., 2013).

At the same time Henry Dreyfuss was making significant strides in usability, Walt Disney was conducting research and development in the realm of user experience design. For this reason, he is frequently referred to as the original user experience designer.

In the 1950s, Disney expanded into the amusement park industry, and in July 1955, Disneyland opened its doors in Anaheim, California. Every detail of the park was meticulously planned to deliver an immersive experience. He called his staff "Imagineers" and provided them with ten guiding principles, later known as "Mickey's 10 Commandments".

1.2.8 1995: Donald Norman gives UX Design a Name

The first individual to hold "UX" in his job title was cognitive scientist Donald Norman, who became Apple's User Experience Architect in the early 1990s. He coined the phrase "user experience design" to describe UX in its entirety. As Norman explained, "I wanted to cover all aspects of a person's experience with a system, including industrial design, graphics, the interface, the physical interaction, and the manual. I thought human interface and usability were too narrow, so I came up with the term."

One of the foundational works of UX design is Norman's 1988 book The *Psychology of Everyday Things*, later revised as *The Design of Everyday Things*. This influential text examines numerous essential design components, including affordances, signifiers, feedback, and more (Norman, 1988, 1990).

1.2.9 From 2000 to the Modern World

The development of UI/UX design since 2000 reflects both the rapid pace of technological advancement and the evolving demands of consumers. In 2007, the launch of the first iPhone marked the beginning of a revolutionary user experience and the birth of the modern smartphone. With its intuitive touch interface, the iPhone introduced seamless access to apps, messaging, photo sharing, weather updates, and built-in GPS, all at the tap of a finger. Since then, not merely a device; it signaled the start of a new era in connectivity and convenience the industry has steadily evolved to deliver more user-friendly, engaging, and inclusive digital experiences. From the era of Web 2.0 and Flash to today's focus on AI, AR/VR, and ethical design, UI/UX has continually adapted to meet changing expectations. As technology continues to advance, UI/UX design will remain a powerful force shaping the way people interact with digital products and services.

1.3 Importance of UI/UX in Digital Products

The significance of user interface (UI) and user experience (UX) design in digital products cannot be overstated. Effective UI/UX design makes digital products more enjoyable and easier to use while greatly enhancing consumer satisfaction. A well-designed user interface attracts and retains users by being consistent, intuitive, and visually appealing. In contrast, a well-designed user experience ensures that the product meets user needs, providing a smooth and efficient journey that reduces frustration and boosts productivity. According to Shashi Shekhar Shukla (2023), UI UX design has a profound impact on the success of digital products including:

Helps Users Achieve Their Goals	Increases User Engagement	Builds User Trust	Increases User Satisfaction	Help Users by Localizing the Product	Provide More Accessibility to Users with Disabilities
Streamlines user journeys to complete tasks efficiently and effectively.	Creates an intuitive and enjoyable experience that encourages continued interaction.	Fosters credibility and reliability through a professional and predictable interface.	Enhances overall user happiness by reducing friction and creating positive interactions.	Adapts the product to a user's local language and culture for greater relevance.	Ensures the product is usable and equitable for people with diverse abilities.

Figure 1.3: Importance of UI/UX in digital products.

1.3.1 Helps Users Achieve their Goals

User interface (UI) and user experience (UX) design are essential for enabling people to accomplish their goals quickly and effectively. With simple controls, clear iconography, and intuitive layouts, a well-designed user interface allows users to navigate a digital product with ease. For example, a well-designed banking app will feature clearly labeled buttons for transactions, account information, and customer support, making it straightforward for users to transfer funds or check their balance. UX design, on the other hand, focuses on the user's complete experience and journey. To better understand the needs, desires, and pain points of their users, UX designers conduct in-depth research. They then create workflows that align with users' goals, often using personas and journey maps, tools that will be explained in the following chapters.

For instance, UX design in an e-commerce app ensures that finding products, adding them to the basket, and completing the transaction are simple reducing the number of steps required to achieve the purchase goal. UI/UX design minimizes friction and removes potential obstacles by prioritizing usability and accessibility. This includes improving load times, ensuring responsiveness on mobile devices, and providing assistive features for users with disabilities. Effective UI/UX design also incorporates feedback mechanisms such as progress indicators and confirmation messages, reassuring users that they are on the right track.

1.3.2 Increases User Engagement

An attractive digital product, much like a successful physical store, is built on a symbiotic relationship between its surface appeal and its underlying functional design. The User Interface (UI) serves as both architecture and interior design; it is the visual presentation, consistent branding, and stylish features that create a strong first impression, drawing users in and building trust. However, this appeal is only sustainable when paired with an outstanding User Experience (UX), which encompasses an intuitive layout, clear navigation, and supportive guidance. UX represents the intelligent, user-centric journey that makes exploring the product simple, efficient, and enjoyable. By seamlessly merging a beautiful, trustworthy interface with a genuinely intuitive and frictionless experience, engagement obstacles are removed. This powerful synergy transforms a product from mere utility into a source of delight, ensuring that users connect with it not only out of necessity but also with loyalty, the ultimate foundation for long-term success.

1.3.3 Builds User Trust

UI (User Interface) and UX (User Experience) design are crucial in establishing user trust in digital products. A well-designed UI contributes to a professional and polished appearance, creating a strong first impression and instilling confidence in users. Consistent design elements, such as fonts, colour palettes, and button styles, convey reliability and attention to detail. An intuitive layout that aligns with user expectations further reassures them that they are engaging with a thoughtfully designed product. UX design builds trust by focusing on the overall experience and ensuring that the product effectively meets user needs. Through thorough research and testing, UX designers identify and resolve pain points, creating a smooth smooth, frustration-free journey. Confidence arises when users feel understood and in control, which is achieved through responsive interactions, logical workflows, and clear navigation. Equally important UX design emphasizes communication and transparency. This includes open feedback channels, accessible customer support, and clear instructions. Progress indicators during processes, such as online purchases or form submissions, help users stay informed and reduce anxiety. Additionally, safeguarding data security and privacy through transparent policies and secure transactions strengthens customer confidence.

By combining a user-centric and transparent UX design with an aesthetically pleasing and consistent UI, digital products can foster a trustworthy environment. Products that inspire trust are more likely to be used repeatedly, increasing customer loyalty and driving long-term success.

1.3.4 Increases User Satisfaction

Designing digital products that are both useful and enjoyable is a central goal of UI (User Interface) and UX (User Experience) design. A well-designed user interface ensures attractive and user-friendly graphics. Clear, visually appealing elements, such as buttons, icons, and typography, make it easier for users to interact with the product. When users can quickly find what they need and understand how to use various features, they feel happier and more in control of their experience.

UX design, by contrast, focuses on the user's overall journey and emotional response. Through usability testing and user research, UX designers gain insights into user preferences and pain points, enabling them to create experiences that meet expectations. This may involve simplifying complex processes, providing helpful feedback, and ensuring accessibility for all users, including those with disabilities. From the first interaction to ongoing use, effective UX design considers every touchpoint, optimizing for convenience and enjoyment. This holistic approach produces a seamless, integrated experience that reduces frustration and enhances satisfaction. For instance, an e-commerce site with a streamlined checkout process, clear product descriptions, and intuitive navigation will not only improve customer satisfaction but also encourage repeat business.

1.3.5 Help Users by Localizing the Product

Users can benefit immensely from UI (User Interface) and UX (User Experience) design when products are localized, making them more relevant and accessible to a global audience. Localization involves adapting a product to meet the linguistic, cultural, and geographic needs of different user groups. This process makes the product feel more familiar and approachable, thereby enhancing consumer satisfaction and overall experience.

Clearness and usability are improved when interface text is translated into the user's regional language. This includes not only the main text but also buttons, labels, error messages, and other interface components. To avoid misunderstandings and align with cultural preferences, icons, images, and color schemes should also be adapted. For instance, selecting colors appropriate to a specific culture is crucial, as different societies may assign different meanings to particular hues. Additionally, localization requires adjusting time zones, date formats, and number formats (such as currency symbols and decimal separators) to conform to local conventions.

Adapting the user experience and interactions to align with cultural norms and expectations is essential. For instance, the appearance and flow of an e-commerce checkout process may need to be adjusted to reflect local purchasing habits. Providing content that resonates with the local audience, such as region-specific promotions, recommendations, and support resources, further enhances relevance and engagement. It is also critical to ensure that the product meets local accessibility standards and accommodates users with disabilities. This may include features such as right-to-left text support for languages like Arabic and Hebrew.

Users are more likely to find the product easy to use when it reflects their language and cultural standards. A localized product appeals to a wider audience, leading to higher adoption rates across different regions. Users are also more inclined to trust and remain loyal to a product that acknowledges and respects their cultural and geographical demands. Providing a localized product can distinguish a company from competitors that do not offer such personalized services. Organizations that prioritize localization in UI and UX design deliver a more inclusive and enjoyable experience for users worldwide, resulting in greater engagement, satisfaction, and long-term loyalty.

1.3.6 Provide More Accessibility to Users with Disabilities

UI (User Interface) and UX (User Experience) design play a crucial role in making digital products accessible to users with disabilities. Accessibility ensures that all individuals, including those with physical, cognitive, and sensory impairments, can effectively use and interact with a product. By embedding accessibility into UI/UX design, companies can create inclusive experiences that serve a diverse audience.

- Readable Text: Use clear, legible fonts and provide options to adjust text size and contrast. Ensure sufficient contrast between text and background colors to support users with visual impairments.

- Keyboard Navigation: Design interfaces to be fully navigable via keyboard, enabling users with motor impairments to access all functions without relying on a mouse.

- Alternative Text for Images: Provide descriptive alt text for images, icons, and other non-text elements so screen readers can convey information to visually impaired users.

- Accessible Color Choices: Avoid relying solely on color to communicate information. Use patterns, labels, or icons alongside color to ensure that colourblind users can interpret content.

- Clear and Consistent Navigation: Create intuitive, consistent navigation structures that are easy to understand, helping users with cognitive disabilities avoid confusion.
- Form Accessibility: Ensure forms are accessible by including clear labels, instructions, and error messages. Use ARIA (Accessible Rich Internet Applications) landmarks to enhance form accessibility.
- Voice and Gesture Support: Incorporate voice control and gesture-based navigation for users with mobility impairments, offering alternative ways to interact with the product.
- Captioning and Transcripts: Provide captions for videos and transcripts for audio content to assist users with hearing impairments. Ensure multimedia content is accessible through multiple sensory modalities.

By prioritizing accessibility in UI and UX design, companies can deliver products that are more usable, inclusive, and appealing to a diverse user base. This commitment not only enhances user satisfaction but also demonstrates social responsibility and ethical design practices.

1.4 Steps for Design Process

The design process for UI (User Interface) and UX (User Experience) consists of several stages, each essential for creating effective and user-centered digital products. According to Fathima (2023), the user experience design process can be outlined in ten steps, as illustrated in Figure 1.4.

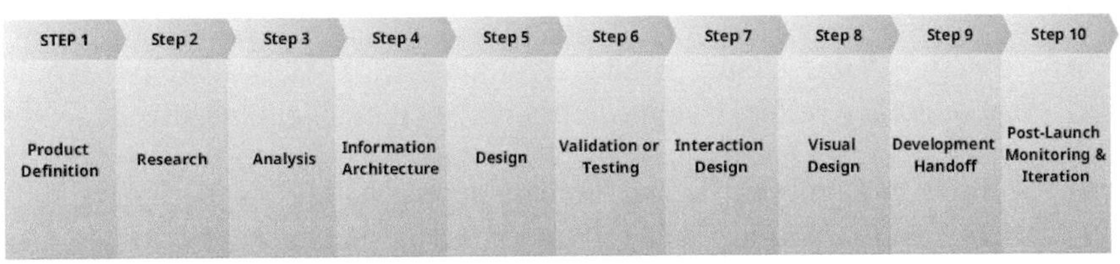

Figure 1.4: Design process for UI and UX.

1.4.1 Product Definition

The first step in the user design process is called "Product Definition." During this stage, the team gathers user needs within the context of the business. This step establishes the product's vision, outlines its essential features, and sets the key metrics for success. By answering the fundamental questions, What is the product? Who is it for? Why does it matter?, product definition creates a clear, shared roadmap that guides all subsequent decisions in design, development, and marketing, ensuring the final outcome effectively meets both user needs and business objectives.

It is essential to communicate the needs to UI/UX designers before beginning any work. The Design Team, Business Manager, and Product Manager are responsible for this stage. The entire team should collaborate with users in their environment, assessing requirements within the framework of their business operations. The main outputs of this phase, use case diagrams, user personas, and user stories, are explained in the following chapters. Common tools used at this stage include Confluence or Notion for documentation, and Miro or Mural for collaborative workshops.

1.4.2 Research

The most important component of the design process is UI/UX research, which provides the foundation for developing user-centred solutions. Conducted before the design phase, research enables designers to thoroughly examine the existing system, understand user behavior, and identify areas for improvement. Without sufficient research, even the most aesthetically pleasing interfaces may fail to meet user needs or business objectives. Three key tasks are performed during the research phase to ensure a well-informed design plan:

- Competitive Analysis: Designers must identify their rivals, study their products, evaluate strengths and weaknesses, and determine opportunities to differentiate.
- Domain Analysis: A comprehensive review the current domain should consider technical limitations, industry trends, and user demographics.
- Strategy Assessment: Evaluating competitor tactics helps predict outcomes and refine design choices based on practical insights.

In addition to competitive and domain research, UI/UX designers must stay current with emerging design trends such as voice user interfaces, micro-interactions, and dark mode. They should also adhere to fundamental design principles, including usability, consistency, and accessibility. Compliance is supported by consulting online design catalogues and established guidelines, such as WCAG (Web Content Accessibility Guidelines), Google's Material Design, and Apple's Human Interface Guidelines. The most commonly used tools include UserTesting for recruiting participants, SurveyMonkey or Google Forms for surveys, and Airtable for synthesizing and organizing research data.

1.4.3 Analysis

The foundation for developing a product's design strategy lies in the information gathered during the UI/UX research phase. Designers often create personas and experience maps, two essential tools that bridge research and design by analyzing user data, industry trends, and competitor benchmarks. By visualizing end users and their journeys, these artefacts ensure that the final product meets practical requirements.

Personas are fictitious, data-driven representations of the product's intended users. They are built from research findings such as demographics, behaviors, pain spots, and goals. By establishing these profiles, designers gain a clearer knowledge of who will use the product and why. Personas humanise abstract data, enabling the design team to tailor interfaces, features, and interactions to real-world expectations. This process ensures that the finished product is not only functional but also intuitive and easy to understand for its target audience.

Once personas are defined, experience maps can help describe how users will interact with the product. These visual diagrams outline sequential interactions, from initial discovery to task completion. Experience maps highlight pain points, emotional touchpoints, and opportunities for improvement, resulting in a smoother and more user journey. For example, a User Journey Map: E-Commerce App Onboarding is illustrated in Table 1.2. Designers refine these maps by collaborating with clients during the product definition stage, ensuring they reflect real-world usage scenarios. This approach guarantees that the final design is both user-friendly and aligned with business objectives. Common tools used for collaborative sorting and mapping include Miro and Figma's FigJam.

1.4.4 Information Architecture

Information architecture (IA) forms the foundation of every successful digital product, and UI/UX designers devote significant effort to refining. A well-structured IA organizes and prioritizes content so that users can navigate effortlessly, reducing cognitive load and enhancing overall usability. When executed effectively, it enables users to achieve their goals intuitively, leading to greater engagement and satisfaction.

- Identify the content hierarchy: The first step in developing effective IA is to establish a clear hierarchy. This requires a thorough content audit to assess existing resources and uncover gaps. Content should be logically structured around user needs and behaviors.

- Create sitemaps: Designers then build sitemaps to visualize the product's framework including navigation paths and content relationships. Tools such as Lucidchart help refine these plans before development begins.

Table 1.2: User journey map: E-Commerce app onboarding.

Stage	User Action	Pain Points	Emotion
Discover	Sees ad/recommendation. "Looks interesting."	Vague value proposition. Quality concerns.	Curiosity
Download	Installs and opens app.	Slow download. Excessive permissions.	Impatience
Sign Up	Faces registration form. "Another account?"	No social login. Complex password rules.	Frustration
Onboard	Asked for preferences/sizes.	Mandatory, cannot skip. Feels tedious.	Resistance
Browse	Searches for specific item. "Where is it?"	Poor search. Confusing navigation.	Confusion
Evaluate	Checks product details. "Right size? Quality?"	No size guide. Few/unreliable reviews.	Doubt
Checkout	Proceeds to purchase.	Hidden shipping costs. Long/complex form.	Anger
Purchase	Enters payment details. "Is this secure?"	Security concerns. No guest checkout.	Anxiety
Post-Purchase	Awaits confirmation/shipping.	No immediate email/tracking. Poor support.	Worry
Outcome	Product arrives.	Item mismatch/ poor quality. Hard returns.	Delight or Disappointment

- Validate navigation: Finally, navigation must be tested to ensure alignment with user expectations. Techniques like tree testing and card sorting provide valuable insights. Platforms such as Optimal Workshop reveal how easily users locate information, allowing adjustments before final implementation.

Even with careful planning, information architecture (IA) design presents challenges. One major difficulty is information overload, which occurs when arises when users are confronted with too many choices at once. The solution lies in leveraging analytics to prioritize frequently accessed content while progressively revealing supplementary information. Another common issue is imprecise terminology, labels or classifications that confuse rather than guide. This can be resolved by testing terminology with real users through surveys or A/B testing to ensure clarity. Addressing these issues helps minimize frustration and reduce abandonment later.

Even the most visually appealing designs can be undermined by a poorly structured interface, leaving users confused and dissatisfied. In contrast, a well-designed IA serves as an invisible guide, seamlessly directing users toward their goals. IA is not merely about menus and sitemaps; it is about crafting a logical flow that feels intuitive. By investing in strong IA, designers create the foundation for products that are not only functional but also genuinely enjoyable to navigate. Tools such as Optimal Workshop (for card sorting and tree testing) and Figma or Whimsical (for sitemaps and flow diagrams) are widely used at this stage.

1.4.5 Design

After extensive research, persona development, and information architecture planning, the UI/UX design process enters its most tangible stage: transforming concepts into visual reality. This phase applies systematic design principles to translate abstract ideas into functional, aesthetically pleasant interfaces.

The design step begins with sketching, where designers convert ideas into rough, hand-drawn visuals. These quick sketches provide a low-fidelity way to explore layout options navigation flows, and key elements without committing to details too early. By rapidly iterating on paper, designers can evaluate multiple approaches and select the most promising direction before moving to digital tools. Sketching fosters creativity and alignment, ensuring the team shares a clear vision from the outset.

Once sketches are complete, designers move on to creating wireframes, low-fidelity blueprints that outline the product's structure. Wireframes establish the foundation of the design by defining the hierarchy of elements, content placement, and user pathways. They emphasize functionality over aesthetics, ensuring the interface is intuitive before visual details are introduced. Tools such as Figma, Balsamiq, and Adobe XD streamline this process, enabling teams to collaborate and iterate more effectively.

Once wireframes are approved the next step is prototyping, creating a live, interactive model of the product. Prototypes simulate how users will engage with the interface, incorporating transitions, animations, and microinteractions. This stage emphasizes the feel of the design, helping identify usability issues before development begins. Tools such as InVision and Proto.io enable designers to build clickable prototypes that stakeholders and users can test, providing vital feedback for refinement.

The process culminates in design specifications, comprehensive documents that detail user flows, task flows, and stylistic guidelines. These specifications include typography, color palettes, spacing rules, and interaction patterns, ensuring consistency across devices. By bridging the gap between design and development, specifications allow engineers to implement the product accurately while preserving the intended user experience. Tools like Figma, Sketch, and Adobe XD are commonly used to create wireframes, mockups, and prototypes throughout this stage.

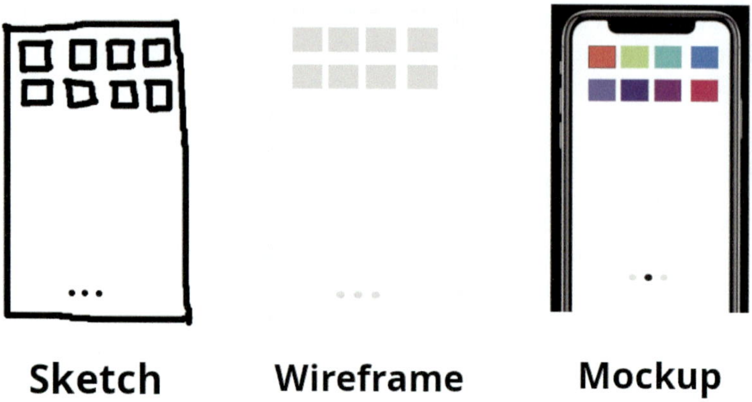

Figure 1.5: *sketch → black/white wireframe → colored mockup.*

1.4.6 Validation or Testing

The validation phase is where theory meets reality: real users interact with the design, revealing both its strengths and weaknesses. As Usability-Testing.org explains, "Usability testing is the practice of putting designs to the test with real people to gather information about the user experience and how difficult or easy it is to use the product." Whether applied to a website, mobile app, or prototype, this process uncovers critical insights that shape the final product.

The primary goal of usability testing is to assess how intuitive and efficient a digital product is. By observing users as they complete tasks, designers can identify pain points moments of uncertainty, navigation breakdowns, or experiences that fail to meet expectations. This approach not only highlights UX flaws but also provides actionable data to refine the design before launch. Beyond improving usability, early testing reduces development costs by catching issues before they become expensive post-release fixes. Usability testing typically follows two approaches:

- Moderated Testing: A UX researcher guides participants through tasks, asking questions and analyzing behavior in real time. This method yields rich qualitative feedback but requires more resources.
- Unmoderated Testing: Users complete tasks independently, often remotely, while platforms such as UserTesting or Lookback record interactions. This scalable and cost-effective method generates quantitative data and broader user insights.

Even the most well-researched designs risk alienating users if they are not tested for usability. Testing validates assumptions, ensures accessibility, and ultimately boosts conversion rates by reducing friction. By incorporating feedback early on, teams can create solutions that are not only functional but also intuitive, turning first-time users into loyal advocates. Tools such as UserTesting or Lookback enable remote testing, while platforms like Figma and InVision are commonly used to share clickable prototypes with participants.

1.4.7 Interaction Design

Interaction Design (IxD) shapes the way users engage with digital products. It extends beyond static visuals to define every click, swipe, and gesture, ensuring interactions feel intuitive, responsive, and enjoyable. When executed effectively, IxD elevates functional interfaces into dynamic experiences that delight users.

The process begins with establishing user flows, which map the specific steps users take to complete tasks such as signing up or making a transaction. Tools like FlowMapp help visualize these pathways, ensuring logical seamless navigation. Designers then focus on micro-interactions, small but impactful details such as button hover effects and loading animations. These subtle elements provide instant feedback, making the interface feel more dynamic and responsive. For instance, a button that changes color when pressed reassures users that their action has been successfully registered.

Once interactions are designed, they are brought to life through interactive prototypes created with tools such as Figma or ProtoPie. These prototypes are tested with real users to ensure clarity and ease of use. Accessibility remains a priority, incorporating features like keyboard navigation, screen reader compatibility, and inclusive design standards. Spotify demonstrates this effectively offering seamless transitions when adding songs to playlists, enhancing usability without interruption.

However, interaction design is not without challenges. Overloading users with animations can lead to confusion and frustration. The key is restraint: motion should guide rather than distract. Maintaining consistency across the product is another hurdle. Standardizing interaction patterns, such as uniform button behaviors, helps users build predictable mental models, reducing cognitive load. Commonly used tools for advanced interactive prototypes include Figma (with Smart Animate), ProtoPie, and After Effects.

1.4.8 Visual Design

Visual design is far more than making interfaces look appealing; it is a crucial element that enhances usability while fostering emotional connections with users. Through thoughtful use of typography, color schemes, and layout, visual design transforms functional interfaces into cohesive, engaging experiences. At the core, it stands as an integral aspect of a comprehensive UI/UX strategy, balancing aesthetics with usability.

The first step in our visual design process is to establish a design system, composed of reusable components, style guidelines, and interface patterns. Tools like Storybook help maintain product consistency by ensuring that buttons, cards, and other elements follow standardized design rules. This systematic approach accelerates development and prevents visual fragmentation, which could otherwise confuse consumers.

Choosing the appropriate typography is about more than selecting attractive typefaces; it also defines readability, hierarchy, and tone. For instance, a financial app may use bold, professional fonts to convey security, while a children's app might adopt playful, rounded typefaces to create a sense of fun. Similarly, color psychology shapes user perception: blues inspire trust (common in banking apps), while vibrant oranges suggest energy (often seen in fitness platforms).

Strong visual design weaves brand identity into every detail. It goes beyond simply placing a logo on the screen; encompassing mascots, custom graphics, and even micro-interactions that reflect the brand's personality. Apple exemplifies this approach, reinforcing its premium image through minimalist layouts, generous white space, and carefully controlled color palettes.

Yet, even the most visually appealing design fails if it excludes users. Accessibility must be rigorously evaluated,considering contrast ratios, font sizes, and color-blindness compatibility. Tools like Stark automate these checks, ensuring compliance with WCAG guidelines while preserving aesthetic appeal. Commonly used tools include Figma (for building component libraries), Storybook (for developers to view and maintain design systems), and Stark (for accessibility testing).

1.4.9 Development Handoff

The development handoff marks a critical transition from design to implementation, with pixel-perfect execution determines whether an idea becomes a reality. This stage demands meticulous attention to detail, every spacing rule, interaction behavior, and graphic element must be explicitly defined to minimize confusion. A well-executed handoff bridges the gap between designers and developers, ensuring the final product delivers the intended user experience.

Designers should begin by annotating their work with clear notes that explain the purpose, functionality, and edge cases of UI components. For instance, annotations might specify hover states for buttons or error messages for form fields. These notes serve as a road map for developers, reducing guesswork and minimizing future back-and-forth communication. Tools such as Figma and Adobe XD allow designers to embed comments directly into design files, creating a living document that evolves alongside the project.

Next, provide comprehensive specifications that include color codes, asset exports (icons, images), and precise measurements such as padding, margins, and font sizes. Platforms like Zeplin or Figma's Inspect Mode automate this process by generating style guides and CSS snippets that developers can easily replicate. To illustrate timing and easing curves for animations or complex interactions, supplement these specifications with prototype links or Lottie files.

Even with thorough documentation, questions will inevitably arise. Schedule regular designer-developer syncs to resolve ambiguities quickly. Encourage open communication through pair programming, sprint planning sessions, or Slack discussions. This collaborative approach prevents last-minute surprises and ensures the design intent remains aligned. Tools such as Figma and Zeplin not only generate style code (CSS, etc.) but also provide a shared platform for seamless designer-developer collaboration.

1.4.10 Post-Launch Monitoring and Iteration

Although launching the product is a significant milestone, the journey is far from complete. The real value emerges during post-launch monitoring, which reveals how consumers interact with the product in real-world scenarios, uncovers overlooked issues, and guides ongoing improvements. This stage is essential for staying competitive and ensuring the product evolves to meet user needs.

Begin by using tools such as Google Analytics or Hotjar to track measurable data points like bounce rates, session durations, and conversion rates. These metrics indicate whether users are achieving their goals or encountering obstacles. For instance, a checkout page with a high drop-off rate may signal a design flaw that requires immediate attention. Establishing early baseline metrics provides a foundation for evaluating the impact of future iterations.

Numbers alone do not tell the whole story. Gather qualitative feedback through surveys, user interviews, or in-app tools such as Typeform. Ask open-ended questions to uncover frustrations and desires, for instance, "What almost stopped you from completing your purchase?" Such feedback is invaluable for identifying usability issues or unmet needs that analytics may overlook.

Once data and feedback are gathered, prioritize iterative updates top priority. Address critical defects before focusing on enhancements that align with user needs and business objectives, fix important defects. Instagram exemplifies this approach with features like Stories and Reels, which remain fresh and engaging by evolving based on user feedback and engagement metrics.

Although negative comments can feel discouraging, treat them as valuable input. Focus on actionable insights rather than distractions. For instance, if users express frustration with unclear navigation, explore alternative designs and run A/B tests to identify improvements. Another common challenge is update fatigue. Introducing changes gradually and communicating them transparently through release notes or in-app tutorials, helps prevent users from feeling overwhelmed. Widely used tools include Google Analytics, Amplitude, Hotjar for analytics and heatmaps, as well as Typeform or Intercom for gathering user feedback.

1.5 Conclusion

UI/UX design is a strategic discipline that directly shapes a product's success and user adoption in today's competitive digital market. It highlights the essential relationship between a visually appealing interface (UI) and an intuitive user experience (UX), where aesthetic design must be paired with functional intelligence. Exceptional design is grounded in empathy, continuous research, and real user validation, drawing on human-centred principles that span from ancient ergonomics to modern digital techniques. This approach immediately adds corporate value by fostering user engagement, building trust, enhancing satisfaction, and cultivating long-term loyalty through seamless goal achievement. A methodical, iterative design process, from initial product definition to post-launch refinement, ensures solutions are based on validated insights rather than assumptions, ultimately reducing development costs while enhancing the likelihood of success.

Chapter 2

From Philosophy to Practice: Integrating Human-Centered Design and Design Thinking in UX

User Experience (UX) design is built upon two core foundations: Human-Centered Design (HCD) as its guiding philosophy, and Design Thinking as its structured process. HCD serves as the ethical framework, ensuring a deep focus on human needs and empathy. Design Thinking provides the actionable, iterative steps, Empathize, Define, Ideate, Prototype, and Test, that bring this philosophy to life. Together, this powerful combination reduces bias, mitigates risk through rapid prototyping, and drives innovation. It forms the essential blueprint for creating digital products that are not only functional but also deeply meaningful and user-centric.

2.1 Human-Centered Design

Human-centred design (HCD) is an iterative and empathetic approach that grounds the entire design process in a deep understanding of the people it serves, prioritizing their needs, capabilities, behaviors, and lived experiences. Guided

DOI: 10.1201/9781003715764-2

by core principles of empathy, co-creation, and rapid prototyping, HCD goes beyond solving technical problems. It requires direct engagement with users through methods such as ethnographic research and usability testing to uncover not only their explicit requirements but also their underlying, often unspoken challenges and aspirations. This rigorous, user-informed methodology ensures that the resulting solutions are not only highly usable and effective but also deeply resonant, meaningful, and sustainable in real-world contexts. According to Interaction Design Foundation Interaction Design Foundation - IxDF (2021), four key principles define human-centered design, as illustrated in Figure 2.1.

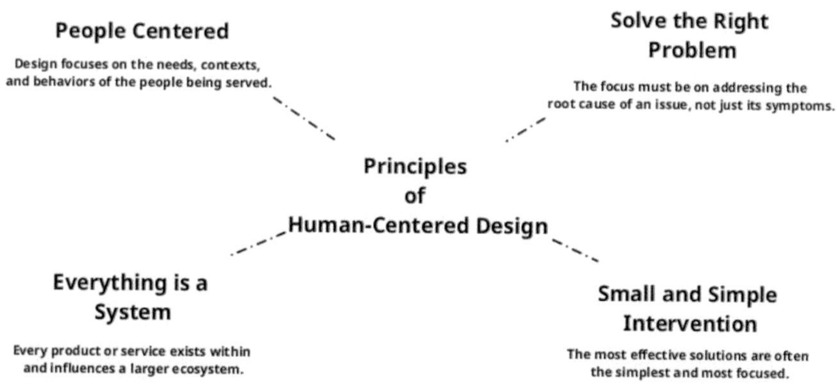

Figure 2.1: The four foundational principles of human-centered design (adapted from Interaction Design Foundation - IxDF (Interaction Design Foundation - IxDF, 2021)).

2.1.1 People Centered

The first principle, Be People-Centered, forms the foundational axiom of Human-Centered Design (HCD). It emphasizes that a design's success is ultimately measured by its positive impact on the person using it, shifting the focus from technological capabilities or business objectives to human needs and values. This requires viewing users as complex individuals with emotions, environments, and goals rather than abstract entities. In UX, neglecting this principle reduces design to mere interface decoration or feature-driven development, risking the creation of products that may be technically impressive but practically unwanted or unusable. Design Thinking operationalizes this principle through its Empathize phase, employing methods such as user interviews, contextual inquiry, and empathy mapping. These activities generate rich qualitative data that serve as foundational evidence for design decisions, ensuring the user's perspective remains central throughout the process.

2.1.2 Solve the Right Problem

The second principle, Solve the Right Problem, underscores the importance of deeply understanding problem before attempting to generate solutions. It requires looking beyond surface-level issues to uncover root causes and authentic user needs. In UX, tackling the wrong problem often leads to wasted resources, product failures, and user frustration, whereas addressing the right problem ensures that design efforts deliver genuine value. Design Thinking puts this principle into practice through its Define phase, using techniques such as affinity mapping, user personas, point-of-view statements, and "How Might We" questions. These methods synthesize research insights into a clear, actionable problem definition, creating alignment and focus so that teams address underlying issues rather than superficial symptoms.

2.1.3 Everything is a System

The third principle, Everything is a System, recognizes that no product exists in isolation. Users engage with designs as part of a broader ecosystem that encompasses other apps, physical objects, social norms, and organizational structures. In UX, neglecting this systemic context can result in fragmented and impractical experiences, whereas designing with the system in mind ensures coherence, consistency, and feasibility. Design Thinking applies this principle as a critical lens across multiple phases, particularly Ideate and Prototype. Techniques such as journey mapping, ecosystem visualization, and prototyping integrations help designers understand and test how their solutions fit within the user's larger environment, leading to holistic and viable outcomes. For instance, designing a fitness app is not just about the app's screens; it requires considering the user's entire fitness ecosystem, their wearable devices, schedule, gym membership, social motivations, and even their kitchen. A successful app integrates seamlessly into this broader system.

2.1.4 Small and Simple Intervention

The fourth principle, Small and Simple Interventions, emphasizes iterative, incremental progress through low-risk, testable actions. It prioritizes learning and adaptation over large-scale execution. In UX, this approach serves as a core risk-management strategy, helping teams avoid costly missteps by validating assumptions early and often with minimal resources. Design Thinking brings this principle to life through the iterative Prototype and Test cycle. Rapid prototyping and usability testing enable teams to create simple artifacts, gather feedback, and refine solutions in tight loops, ultimately building toward a validated product shaped by real user input rather than untested assumptions.

2.2 Design Thinking

While the principles of Human-Centered Design (HCD) provide a vital ethical and conceptual framework, they require a structured process to be effectively applied in practice. This is the role of Design Thinking, which offers a concrete, phased approach to executing human-centered design. According to IDEO's Tim Brown, Design Thinking is 'a human-centered approach to innovation.' This highlights a crucial point: Design Thinking is an approach derived from the philosophy of HCD. Brown explains that it 'draws from the designer's toolkit to merge the demands of people, the possibilities of technology, and the requirements for economic success'. This integration addresses the central challenge of modern user experience, and Design Thinking provides the systematic process to navigate it, helping teams in 'finding the optimal balance of feasibility, viability, and desirability' that defines a successful product.

Based on the principles outlined by Christoph Meisel and Harry Leifer of the Hasso-Plattner-Institute of Design at Stanford University, Design Thinking is guided by four core rules that enable its human-centered approach. These rules form the operational backbone of the methodology, ensuring that innovation remains deeply rooted in human needs and real-world contexts.

2.2.1 Human-Centric

The foundational principle of Design Thinking is its human-centricity, a direct operationalization of the HCD 'People-Centered' principle that ensures the methodology never loses sight of its core focus. This approach places user's needs, experiences, and behaviors at the heart of the entire development process. It moves beyond assumptions by employing empathy to deeply understand users' thoughts, emotions, and challenges. The ultimate goal is to integrate these insights into every design decision, resulting in products and services that are not only functional but also genuinely make users' lives easier, more productive, and more meaningful.

2.2.2 Ambiguity

Ambiguity is a fundamental principle of Design Thinking because it reflects the nature of complex, human-centric problems the methodology seeks to address. These "wicked problems" lack clear definitions or single correct answers, and embracing their inherent ambiguity prevents designers from arriving at premature or biased solutions. Rather than viewing ambiguity as a barrier, design thinkers treat uncertainty as a creative opportunity. Safeguards such as timeboxing and divergent/convergent thinking help teams explore this space constructively and avoid analysis paralysis. The process provides a structured framework for navigating uncertainty, using empathy to build understanding, prototyping to make ideas tangible, and iteration to learn from users. In this way, ambiguity is transformed from a paralyzing threat into a powerful engine of innovation, driving solutions that are deeply resonant and effective.

2.2.3 Redesign

The 'Re-design' philosophy recognizes that few products are created entirely from scratch. Most design work involves improving existing solutions, whether digital products, services, or physical objects. This mindset relieves designers of the pressure to achieve "genius" originality and instead emphasizes the practical, meaningful task of incremental enhancement driven by user feedback and evolving contexts. A redesign is a strategic and iterative process of improving an existing product, service, or system by re-evaluating and reshaping its structure, functionality, and appearance. Unlike superficial cosmetic updates, a meaningful redesign addresses deeper user needs, technological advancements, and shifting business goals. It begins with a critical assessment of the current design, using data, user feedback, and usability testing to identify shortcomings, and then applies human-centered principles to reimagine the experience. This may involve simplifying complex workflows, enhancing accessibility, integrating new features, or overhauling the visual language to strengthen engagement and usability. Ultimately, a successful redesign is not just about change; it's about thoughtful transformation that adds tangible value, ensuring the solution remains intuitive, effective, and meaningful to its users.

2.2.4 Tangibility

Tangibility is the essential practice of transforming abstract ideas into concrete, experiential forms that can be seen, shared, and tested. It counters ambiguity and miscommunication by turning concepts into sketches, prototypes, or models that align teams and invite authentic user feedback. By giving shape to early ideas, whether through simple wireframes, physical mock-ups, or digital prototypes, tangibility uncovers flaws, reveals opportunities, and reduces the risk of building solutions on untested assumptions. This process keeps design grounded in real human interaction, fostering empathy, encouraging iteration, and ultimately producing products and services that are not only innovative but also deeply resonant and highly usable.

2.3 The Synergy: From Philosophy to Process

While distinct in focus, Human-Centered Design (HCD) and Design Thinking are two halves of a whole. Their relationship can be understood as a hierarchy of application: HCD represents the why and the what, the guiding mindset and principles, while Design Thinking provides the how and the when the activities and sequence. This synergy ensures that the process remains firmly grounded in human needs at every step.

Table 2.1: Comparison of HCD principles and design thinking rules.

Human-Centered Design (HCD) Principles *The "Why" & "What"*	**Design Thinking (DT) "Rules"** *The "How" & "When"*
The ethical & philosophical foundation. Defines the core values for designing for people.	The process & methodology. Provides the structured activities to execute the HCD philosophy.
To ensure solutions are **meaningful, usable, and sustainable** for the human experience.	To provide a **repeatable, collaborative process** for innovating and solving complex problems.
A **mindset** and a set of guiding values. It answers *"What should we believe in?"*	A **toolkit** and a set of actionable steps. It answers *"How should we proceed?"*
People-Centered: The foundational axiom that success is measured by human impact.	**The Human Rule:** A directive to always ground activities in user needs throughout the process.
Solve the Right Problem: Emphasizes deep problem diagnosis to address root causes.	**Embrace Ambiguity:** Empowers teams to navigate uncertainty without jumping to premature solutions.
Everything is a System: A lens for understanding a design's broader ecosystem.	**The Re-design Rule:** The mindset for working within and improving upon existing contexts.
Small & Simple Interventions: A principle advocating for learning through low-cost actions.	**The Tangibility Rule:** The method for executing interventions by making ideas concrete.

As illustrated in Table 2.1, each HCD principle is operationalized through a corresponding Design Thinking rule. This integrated framework ensures that every stage of the Design Thinking process is guided by the human-centric philosophy of HCD.

To visualize this integrated framework, see Figure 2.2, which demonstrates how the four principles of HCD directly inform and guide the five stages of the Design Thinking process. For instance, the "People Centered" principle is not a vague ideal; it is actively applied during the "Empathize" stage through user interviews and observation. Likewise, the "Small and Simple Interventions" principle is realized in the iterative loop between "Prototype" and "Test." This model ensures that the strategic, human-centric philosophy of HCD drives every tactical step within Design Thinking.

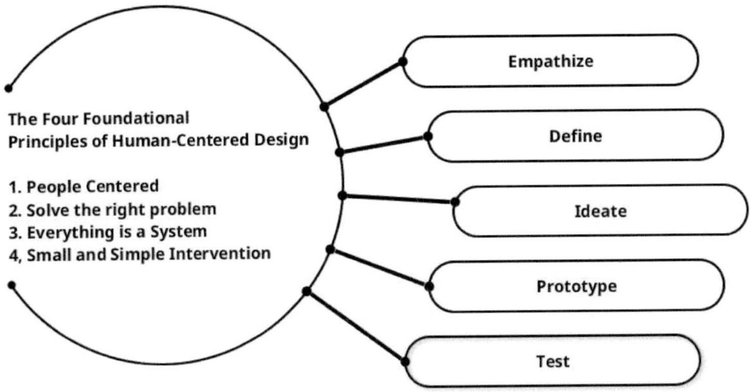

Figure 2.2: The integrated framework: How HCD principles guide the design thinking process.

2.4 Stages of Design Thinking

The phases of Design Thinking provide a structured framework for tackling complex challenges from a human-centered perspective. While institutions may adopt slightly varying numbers of stages (five, six, or seven), the underlying principle remains the same. The most widely recognized model, developed by Stanford's Hasso Plattner Institute of Design (d.school), outlines five key steps (Sonowal, 2025). It is important to note that these phases form an iterative, non-linear cycle rather than a rigid, step-by-step process. As teams develop and refine their ideas, they frequently revisit earlier stages to strengthen and evolve their concepts.

Figure 2.3 illustrates the five-stage Design Thinking process, a nonlinear, iterative framework for addressing complex challenges from a human-centered

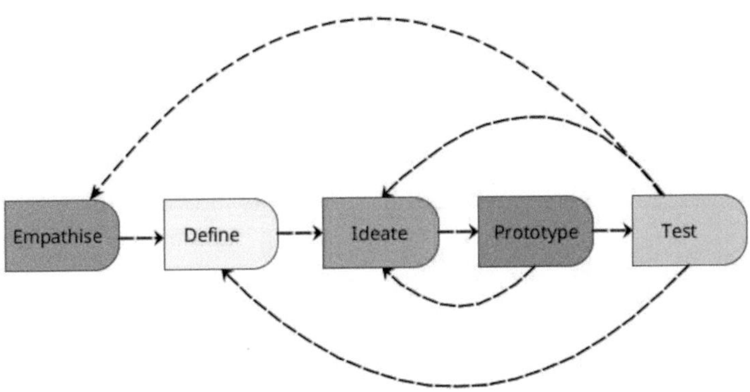

Figure 2.3: Five stages of design thinking process.

perspective. The cycle begins with Empathize, where designers seek to deeply understand users' experiences and needs. It then progresses to Define, in which insights are synthesized into a clear problem statement. In the Ideate stage, teams generate a wide range of creative solutions, which are subsequently developed into tangible artifacts during Prototype, making ideas testable. Finally, in the Test stage, user feedback is gathered to refine solutions and uncover new insights, often prompting a return to earlier phases for further improvement. This iterative cycle underscores the importance of continuous learning, adaptability, and empathy at every stage to ensure meaningful and effective outcomes.

2.4.1 Empathize

The primary purpose of the Empathize stage is to move beyond preconceptions and develop a deep, intimate understanding of the people for whom the design is created. This stage directly enacts the HCD principle of 'Being People-Centered. By stepping into users' shoes, designers gain insight into their experiences, emotional landscapes, motivations, and unspoken obstacles. It represents the core effort of human-centered design, ensuring that all subsequent decisions are grounded in the user's real-world experience rather than the designer's assumptions or biases.

The Empathize stage serves as the foundational research step in the design process. Its purpose is to develop a deep, empathetic understanding of the user's world by gathering rich, qualitative insights. This is primarily accomplished through four core methods of empathetic research: Direct Observation (studying users in their natural context), Skilled Interviews (open-ended conversations to uncover motivations), Surveys (collecting both quantitative and qualitative data), and Focus Groups (facilitating discussions to explore diverse perspectives).

The 5 Whys is a simple yet effective iterative technique used to explore the cause-and-effect relationships underlying a problem. Its primary goal is to identify the root cause by repeatedly asking the question "Why?", typically five times, or until the underlying issue is uncovered. Consider a scenario where people are struggling to use a new smart coffee maker. The observation is: "Users are not making coffee successfully on the first try." The 5 Whys Process:

1. Why are users not making coffee successfully on the first try?

   Answer: Because they are not adding water to the machine.

2. Why are they not adding water?

   Answer: Because they cannot find where to put the water.

3. Why can't they find where to put the water?

   Answer: Because the water reservoir is hidden behind a panel that appears solid and has no visible markings.

4. Why is the reservoir hidden behind a solid, unmarked panel?

   Answer: Because the industrial designer wanted the machine to have a "clean, minimalist look."

5. Why did prioritizing a 'minimalist look' make the machine unusable?

   Answer (Root Cause): Because the design team prioritized aesthetics over usability and failed to test the physical design with users.

Modern technology has significantly enhanced empathic research. Remote, recorded user interviews can now be conducted through digital platforms such as UserTesting[1] and Lookback[2], which capture nuanced verbal and nonverbal cues from anywhere in the world. Tools like Dovetail[3] and Miro[4] enable teams to collaboratively synthesize large volumes of qualitative data, transcribing interviews, tagging insights, and identifying themes, to uncover patterns efficiently. In addition, behavioral analytics platforms such as Hotjar provide objective data by showing how users naturally interact with a product through heatmaps and session recordings. These often reveal a disconnect between what users say and what they actually do.

The outcome is a profound, empathetic awareness of the user's environment, strengthened and validated by technology. This is more than a report; it becomes a shared conviction within the design team. By combining human stories with behavioral data and pattern analysis, teams gain a comprehensive and evidence-based perspective. This rich foundation of empathy serves as the critical filter for all future ideas, ensuring that the design process consistently produces solutions that are truly meaningful and impactful for users.

2.4.2 Define

The primary objective of the Define stage is to compile and interpret the unprocessed data gathered during the Empathize stage. This step involves moving from observations to a precise, human-centered problem statement. By drawing on user quotations, behaviors, pain points, and insights, the team transforms disparate data into a clear and actionable description of the core problem that must be addressed. The Define stage ensures that everyone on the team aligned and working toward the same goal by providing focus and clarity. In essence, it is where the team strives to 'Solve the Right Problem', synthesizing raw empathy into a concise, actionable problem statement.

During this stage, designers collaboratively analyze their research findings to uncover patterns, themes, and underlying needs. Techniques such as empathy

[1] `https://www.usertesting.com/`
[2] `https://www.lookback.com/`
[3] `https://dovetail.com/`
[4] `https://miro.com/`

maps Gibbons, S. (2018), user personas McCay, A. (2024), and customer journey maps (Mann, N., 2023) are employed to organize and visualize the data. The key outcome is the formulation of a clear problem statement, often expressed as a "How Might We" (HMW) question. This question framing positions the challenge as an opportunity inspiring ideation while keeping the process firmly grounded in the authentic needs and desires of users.

Technology plays a critical role in structuring and refining problem definition. Digital collaboration platforms such as Miro (is a visual workspace for innovation that empowers distributed teams to collaborate and build)[5], Mural (is an AI-powered visual collaboration platform that enables teams to ideate, align, and execute customer-led strategies in an interactive, shared space)[6], and Google Jamboard (a tool for real-time collaboration that allows students to share ideas and resources both in-class and remotely)[7] enable distributed teams to synthesize insights in real time, clustering observations and co-creating affinity diagrams. AI-powered tools such as sentiment analysis APIs, can process large volumes of qualitative feedback to detect recurring emotional tones or frequently mentioned topics. Additionally, data visualization platforms like Tableau can be integrated to highlight behavioral patterns observed during user tests, adding quantitative clarity to qualitative insights.

The output of the Define stage is a clearly articulated, compelling problem statement, often supported by user personas and journey maps, that guides the entire team. Rooted in user needs, this statement is crafted to be narrow enough to remain manageable yet broad enough to allow creative freedom. It serves as a strategic foundation, ensuring that the subsequent ideation efforts are purposeful, user-informed, and aligned with a meaningful goal. Without a strong definition, ideation risks becoming misdirected; with it, creativity gains both intention and direction.

2.4.3 Ideate

The primary goal of the Ideate stage is to generate a wide, diverse, and innovative range of potential solutions to the problem defined in the previous stage. It is a dedicated space for expansive, creative thinking where the emphasis is on quantity and variety rather than immediate feasibility. The objective is to move beyond obvious answers, challenge assumptions, and explore novel directions that may lead to breakthrough ideas for addressing user's core needs. This act of making ideas tangible directly applies the HCD principle of 'Small and Simple Interventions', enabling continuous learning and reducing risk before any major investment is made.

[5]https://miro.com/

[6]https://www.mural.co

[7]https://sites.google.com/eastpennsd.org/epsdtech/elementary/google/google-jamboard

This stage employs structured brainstorming techniques to spark creativity and encourage free thinking. Methods such as mind mapping, worst possible idea (to reduce pressure and inspire reverse thinking), SCAMPER, and brainwriting are commonly used. The fundamental rule is to defer judgment, no idea is too bold, too costly, or too unconventional at the outset. This approach creates a psychologically safe environment where participants can build on one another's thoughts, often leading to unexpected and more innovative concepts.

Technology further enhances the ideation process by enabling collaboration and managing the flow of ideas. Digital whiteboarding tools like Miro, Mural, and Jamboard allow distributed teams to brainstorm visually and in real time, providing expansive canvases for notes, sketches, and diagrams. AI-powered ideation platforms, such as ChatGPT or IdeaFlip, can serve as brainstorming partners, generating prompts, suggesting alternatives, and helping to overcome creative blocks. These tools help capture, organize, and visualize large volumes of ideas efficiently, ensuring that no concept is overlooked.

The output of the Ideate stage is a broad portfolio of potential solutions, from incremental improvements to revolutionary concepts. The team does not conclude this stage with a single idea but with a rich repository of possibilities. These ideas are then systematically reviewed, organized, and refined through voting, discussion, and selection criteria (e.g., feasibility, desirability, impact) to identify the most promising candidates for prototyping. This ensures that the transition to the next stage is informed, strategic, and well-prepared for tangible exploration.

2.4.4 Prototype

The primary goal of the Prototype stage is to transform abstract ideas from the Ideate phase into tangible, experiential representations. This stage directly reflects the HCD principle of 'Small and Simple Interventions' by producing low-fidelity, inexpensive artefacts. The purpose is not to build a finished product but to learn, communicate, and validate assumptions quickly and efficiently before significant resources are invested.

During this stage, designers create simplified versions of the product or specific features using methods suited to the nature of the idea. This can range from paper sketches and cardboard models for physical products to clickable digital mockups built in tools such as Figma[8] or Adobe XD[9] for apps and websites. Storyboards and role-playing are often used to prototype services or experiences. The emphasis is on and simplicity, capturing core functionality or interaction to elicit meaningful feedback.

[8] `https://www.figma.com`
[9] `https://adobexdplatform.com/`

Technology dramatically accelerates and enhances prototyping. Digital design tools like Figma, Sketch, and Adobe XD enable rapid creation of high-fidelity, interactive mockups without the need for code. For physical products, 3D printing and laser cutting allow fast, cost-effective production of tangible models. Augmented reality (AR) and virtual reality (VR) tools let users experience spaces or interfaces immersively early in the process, making it possible to test complex ideas in realistic contexts long before development begins.

The output of the Prototype stage is one or more tangible artifacts designed explicitly for testing. These prototypes serve as conversation starters with users and stakeholders, making ideas concrete and accessible. The insights gained from these interactions, what works, what is misunderstood, feed directly into the Test stage. This iterative cycle of building and learning ensures that the design evolves in response to real human feedback, reducing risk and steadily converging on solutions that are both desirable and usable.

2.4.5 Test

The primary goal of the Test stage is to gather authentic feedback from users by placing prototypes into their hands and observing how they interact with them. This stage is not a final exam or a sign-off; rather, it is a structured learning opportunity to validate assumptions, identify usability issues, and uncover deeper insights into user needs and behaviors. The focus is on refining the solution and, when necessary, redefining the problem itself based on real-world evidence. This iterative cycle of building and testing represents the practical application of the HCD principle of 'Small and Simple Interventions, enabling continuous learning and minimizing the risk of developing the wrong solution.

During this stage, designers observe users as they engage with prototypes in realistic scenarios, encouraging them to think aloud and share their impressions, frustrations, and satisfactions. The emphasis is on listening and observing rather than persuading or explaining. Feedback is collected systematically through notes, recordings, and structured observations, then analyzed for patterns and critical insights. This process often uncovers gaps between the designer's intent and the user's actual experience, providing clear guidance for improvement.

Technology enables testing to be more scalable, precise, and insightful. Remote testing platforms such as UserTesting.com and Lookback.io allow feedback to be gathered from diverse users across geographies, recording screens, voices, and facial expressions for detailed analysis. Heatmapping and analytics tools such as Hotjar or FullStory can be integrated into digital prototypes to track interactions quantitatively, revealing where users click, hesitate, or disengage. Survey tools such as Typeform and SurveyMonkey help quantify user reactions, while collaboration platforms like Dovetail support teams in thematically synthesizing qualitative feedback and working together more effectively.

The output of the Test stage is not a "finished" product but a clear set of insights and actionable recommendations. These findings often send the team back to earlier stages, refining the prototype, generating new ideas, redefining the problem, or even revisiting user empathy. This iterative loop of building, testing, and learning ensures that the solution evolves in response to real human feedback. Testing transforms subjective opinions into evidence-based design decisions, significantly reducing risk and aligning the final product with what users genuinely need and desire.

2.5 Challenges in Implementation and How to Overcome Them

While a human-centered approach is highly effective, its implementation often presents specific challenges that can impede progress. Achieving success requires proactively identifying and addressing these common pitfalls.

Confirmation Bias

One significant challenge during the empathy phase is confirmation bias, where teams may unconsciously seek information that validates their pre-existing beliefs. To counter this, it is essential to actively recruit a diverse range of users and deliberately pursue disconfirming evidence through open-ended "why" questions.

Analysis Paralysis

Another common obstacle in the analysis paralysis, where teams become stalled in endless research and debate. Preventing this requires time-boxing the phase and employing a "How Might We" (HMW) statement to drive a concrete and actionable problem definition. The HMW statement is a foundational design thinking tool that transitions a team from problem analysis to solution ideation by framing challenges as open-ended, actionable questions. Its deliberate phrasing is key: "How" assumes a solution is possible, "Might" allows exploration without the pressure of being immediately correct, and "We" fosters collaboration. By striking a careful balance between being too broad and too narrow, a well-crafted HMW statement, such as "How might we help users feel confident they will not miss critical messages?", provides a generative scaffold for brainstorming. It avoids prescribing a specific solution, thereby unlocking creative potential and guiding the team toward innovative, human-centered outcomes.

Solutioneering

During ideation, teams often fall into the trap of "solutioneering", jumping to familiar solutions before fully exploring the problem space. To mitigate this, it is important to first enforce a "no bad ideas" rule, encouraging broad thinking, and then apply techniques such as the "Worst Possible Idea" to deliberately disrupt conventional patterns. The "Worst Possible Idea" is a creative brainstorming method designed to overcome mental blocks and challenge the status quo. Instead of seeking good solutions directly, teams are tasked with intentionally generating the most impractical, ineffective, and absurd ideas they can imagine.

Prototype Attachment

Finally, over-investment in prototypes can cause teams to become overly attached to high-fidelity concepts and resistant to critical feedback. The solution is to mandate starting with low-fidelity prototypes and to, consistently remind the team that the goal is to learn and test ideas, not to build a miniature version of the final product.

2.6 Conclusion

The combination of Human-Centered Design (HCD) and Design Thinking provides the foundation for successful User Experience (UX) design. HCD establishes the core principle, ensuring empathetic attention to human needs and contexts, while Design Thinking provides an actionable, iterative framework for translating this principle into practice through stages such as Empathize, Define, Ideate, Prototype, and Test. This synergy systematically channels creativity, reduces bias, and manages risk through rapid prototyping and user feedback. Together, they form a disciplined yet adaptable methodology that enables teams to create digital products balancing user desire, technological feasibility, and financial viability, resulting in solutions that are not only functional but also meaningful.

Chapter 3

Psychology of User Behavior

The Empathy phase of design thinking requires more than good intentions; it demands a concrete understanding of how humans see, think, and act. Building this depth of empathy means grounding the design process in the principles of human psychology. UI/UX design is not merely about aesthetics, it is about ensuring products perform effectively for users. To achieve this, designers must understand the psychology of user behaviour. By examining cognition, emotion, and motivation, they can create interfaces that are more intuitive, engaging, and effective. This chapter explores the psychological principles that underpin successful UI/UX design and demonstrates how to apply them to enhance user experiences.

3.1 A Framework for Design Psychology

To systematically explore these principles, a framework organized around three core aspects of human cognition can be applied: perception, decision-making, and action & motivation. This tripartite model provides designers with a structured approach to understanding and addressing user needs across different levels of interaction.

DOI: 10.1201/9781003715764-3

3.1.1 The Three Pillars of Design Psychology

Perception: The Gateway to Understanding

The journey begins with perception, how users initially process and organize visual information. The **Gestalt Principles** form the cornerstone of this pillar, explaining the innate cognitive tendencies that shape how humans perceive relationships between elements, distinguish foreground from background, and automatically group visual information into meaningful patterns. By applying these principles, designers can create interfaces that align with users' natural perceptual tendencies, reducing cognitive load and making interfaces immediately clear and comprehensible.

Decision-Making: Navigating Complexity

Once users perceive the interface, they must decide how to interact with it. This pillar focuses on how the complexity and presentation of choices influence user behavior. **Hick's Law** explains the relationship between the number of choices and the time required to make a decision **Miller's Law** addresses the limitations of working memory and the value of chunking information, and **Jakob's Law** underscores the importance of leveraging existing mental models to align with user expectations. Together, these principles guide designers in structuring information and choices in ways that respect cognitive limitations while building on users' prior knowledge.

Action & Motivation: Driving Engagement

The final pillar addresses both the physical interaction with interfaces and the psychological drivers that encourage task completion. **Fitts's Law** provides a mathematical foundation for understanding physical interaction by modeling the relationship between target size, distance, and acquisition time. The **Von Restorff Effect** explains how distinctive elements capture attention and enhance memory, while the **Zeigarnik Effect** shows how incomplete tasks generate cognitive tension that motivates completion. Together, these principles optimize physical interactions and create psychological incentives for sustained engagement.

3.1.2 An Integrated Approach to Design Analysis

This framework provides more than isolated principles; it offers a comprehensive lens for analyzing and improving digital experiences. Each pillar addresses a distinct phase of user interaction:

- **Perception** principles ensure users can *interpret and understand* the interface
- **Decision-Making** principles ensure users can *navigate* the interface efficiently
- **Action and Motivation** principles ensure users can *interact* effectively and feel compelled to complete tasks

The framework's true strength emerges when principles across different pillars work in concert. For instance, applying Gestalt principles (Perception) to create clear visual groupings reduces the cognitive load measured by Hick's Law (Decision-Making), while strategic use of the Von Restorff Effect (Action & Motivation) highlights the most important actions within those groupings. A well-designed button, for instance, employs Gestalt principles (Proximity, Figure/Ground) to be perceived correctly, adheres to Fitts's Law to enable quick interaction, and leverages the Von Restorff Effect to motivate clicks through salience.

3.2 Gestalt Principles

The human brain's ability to complete an image and perceive something greater than the sum of its parts is a remarkable skill. This explains why faces can often be seen in cracks on sidewalks or patterns in tree leaves. Among the Gestalt principles of visual perception, this concept is one of the most fundamental and significant. Max Wertheimer's 1923 Gestalt rules of perceptual organization were among the most influential early contributions to the theory; however, Wolfgang Köhler's 1920 discussion of Physical Gestalten also introduced important ideas (Ripalda et al., 2020).

Gestalt principles are essential concepts for any designer to understand, regardless of their origin (essays dating back to 1890 discuss them). When applied, they can greatly enhance a design's usability and functionality, as well as its aesthetic appeal.

At its core, Gestalt theory is based on the idea that the human brain strives to simplify and organize complex images or designs with multiple components by unconsciously assembling them into a coherent whole rather than perceiving them as unrelated parts. To better comprehend the world, our brains are naturally inclined to recognize patterns and structures.

Gestalt theory is commonly associated with six key principles: (1) Symmetry and order (also known as prägnanz) (2) Continuity (3) Closure (4) Proximity (5) Figure/ground and (6) Similarity. Gestalt is also linked to more recent concepts, such as common fate (Interaction Design Foundation - IxDF, 2016).

3.2.1 Similarity

Humans naturally group similar things together. According to Gestalt principles, comparable items are visually associated regardless of their proximity. They may be organized by characteristics such as size, shape, or color. In design, similarity can unify disparate elements, while contrast can draw attention to specific features. For this reason, call-to-action buttons are often designed to stand out from the rest of a site by using a contrasting color.

Figure 3.1: Here, the squares are evenly distributed and identical in size, yet our brains instinctively group them by colour.

Using similarity in UX design helps users quickly identify which elements are related. For instance, the similarity principle makes it easy to scan a list of features that share recurring design elements, such as an icon paired with three to four lines of text. Conversely, altering the design of elements that need emphasis allows them to stand out and appear more significant. Similarity also supports design consistency, for instance, when links are formatted uniformly across a website, helping users understand the site's structure and organization more effectively.

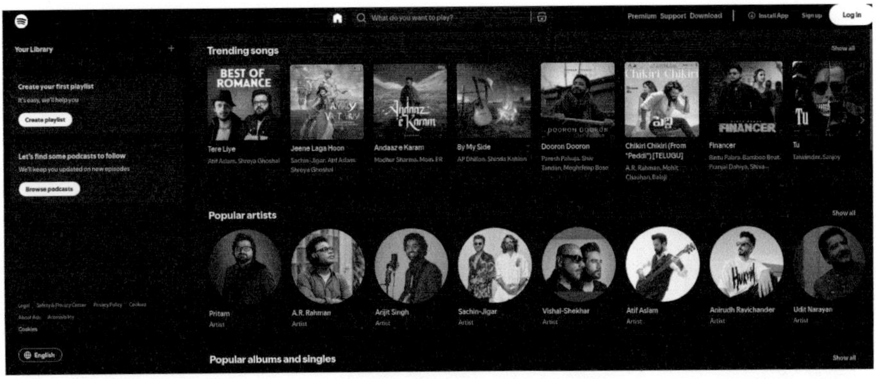

Figure 3.2: The https://open.spotify.com/ interface uses the principle of Similarity to create clear, intuitive groups. The human brain instantly recognises the "Popular artists" as a single list because each entry is styled the same way, a circular icon followed by the word "Artist." Similarly, all the "Trending songs" are grouped in squares because they share an identical layout of a bold title above regular-text artist names. This use of similar visual characteristics allows you to immediately understand the categories and scan the content without confusion.

3.2.2 *Continuation*

The human eye naturally follows the smoothest and most continuous path when observing lines or objects, a phenomenon explained by the Law of Continuity, a fundamental principle of visual perception. This psychological tendency occurs regardless of the actual arrangement or drawing of elements. Within an interface or layout, designers can intentionally guide users' attention along a desired path by leveraging this natural behavior. By understanding and applying this law, designers can create more effective and intuitive visual hierarchies that allow users to move through content with ease.

This principle has a significant impact on digital design. When elements are arranged along a continuous line or curve, users' eyes will naturally follow that path, gliding fluidly from one object to the next. This explains the success of horizontal sliders and carousels, commonly used by e-commerce sites such as Amazon, which display related products in horizontal rows to encourage natural browsing patterns. Because the eye seeks smooth continuations even when elements are physically separated, the continuity effect is so powerful that it can override actual spatial relationships.

3.2.3 *Closure*

Closure illustrates how our brains instinctively fill in gaps in visual information to perceive whole forms, making it one of the most fascinating Gestalt principles. Even when key parts of a design are missing, humans can still recognize familiar

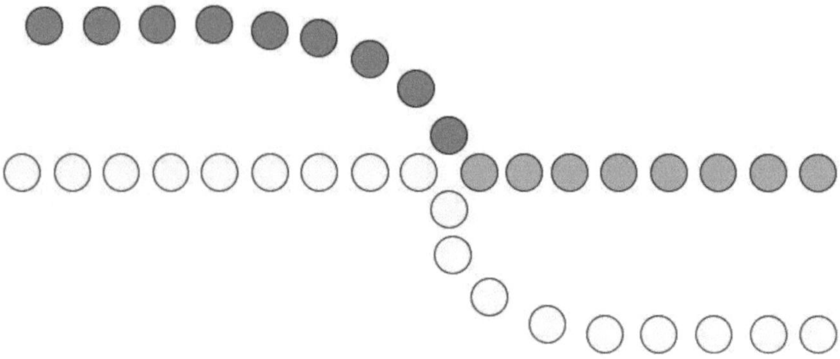

Figure 3.3: The eye automatically follows the straight and curved paths in this figure, maintaining their continuity despite the midline colour changes.

Figure 3.4: Even though a gap breaks the path, human perception does not see two separate, short roads. Instead, the human eye instinctively follows the implied line and curve, connecting the segments into a single, continuous pathway.

shapes thanks to this psychological phenomenon. Closure helps users make sense of fragmented or incomplete visuals by relying on the mind's innate propensity to seek organization and wholeness.

Effective logo design demonstrates the power of closure, where incomplete elements and negative space create clever visual communication. The World Wildlife Fund's iconic panda emblem is a prime example: although much of the outline is absent, human perception effortlessly completes the shape. Similarly, companies such as Adobe and NBC (with its vibrant peacock) to craft simple, distinctive logos that engage viewers through cognitive completion. These designs show how careful use of negative space may result in branding that has a greater impact.

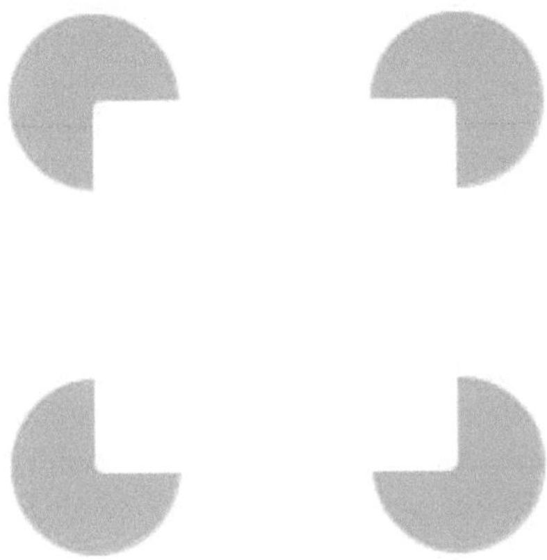

Figure 3.5: Closure.

The Figure 3.5 demonstrates the closure principle in Gestalt psychology, which explains how the brain perceives complete shapes even when portions are missing. In the image, four separate gray shapes each resemble a circle with a quarter removed. Although no square is drawn, their arrangement creates gaps that the mind automatically "fills in," leading viewers to perceive a complete white square at the center. This effect occurs because the visual system seeks patterns and familiar forms, connecting edges to mentally complete the shape. Thus, closure enables us to interpret incomplete visual information as coherent, whole objects.

Closure has important functional applications in UI/UX design that extend beyond aesthetics. A common example is found in sliders and content carousels, where partially visible elements at the screen's margins signal additional content accessible through scrolling. This approach effectively guides user interaction by appealing to our innate drive to complete tasks that appear unfinished. Similarly, skeleton screens and progressive loading animations leverage closure to keep users engaged as content loads, with the brain recognizing emerging patterns before all elements are fully visible.

Figure 3.6: The IBM logo is composed of horizontal lines. The letters "I," "B," and "M" are not fully outlined but formed from stacked rectangles. The human brain instinctively connects these fragments, perceiving the complete letters.

Closure improves user experience by reducing cognitive strain through pattern recognition. When interfaces employ familiar incomplete patterns that users can quickly complete mentally, information processing becomes more efficient. This psychological efficiency leads to smoother navigation and interaction flows. Designers can deliberately apply closure to direct attention, suggest functionality, and establish visual hierarchies that users intuitively understand.

3.2.4 Proximity

Proximity is a key Gestalt principle that explains how humans perceive relationships between elements based on their spatial closeness. When two objects are placed near each other, the brain instinctively interprets them as belonging together or sharing a connection. This principle operates along a continuum; the strongest associations occur between overlapping elements, while simply grouping items within the same general area still produces noticeable connections.

One of the most critical applications of proximity appears in form design. When labels are placed too far from their corresponding input fields, users struggle to associate them correctly. Positioning labels immediately adjacent to their fields (typically 4–8 pixels above or beside them) while adding greater spacing (16–24 pixels) between different sections creates clear visual relationships. For example, a registration form might group "First Name" and "Last Name" fields closer together while placing them farther from the "Email" field below. This subtle spacing difference helps users process form structures more efficiently and with less effort.

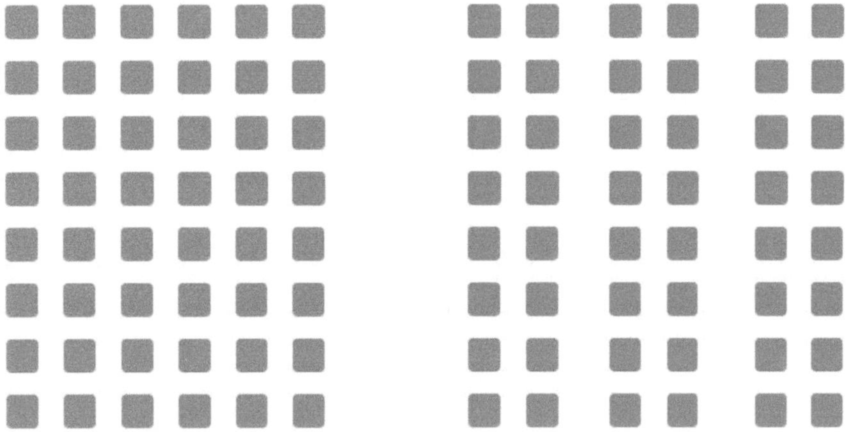

Figure 3.7: Though the elements are identical, their spacing alone makes us perceive the right-side groups as three distinct clusters.

3.2.5 *Figure/Ground*

The figure/ground principle is one of Gestalt psychology's most intriguing concepts, describing how the human brain instinctively separates visual elements into foreground (figure) and background (ground). When viewing an image or interface, attention is naturally drawn to certain elements while others recede. This principle becomes especially compelling in cases of ambiguous figure/ground relationships, where the same visual features can be interpreted in multiple ways depending on which parts the viewer perceives as foreground or background.

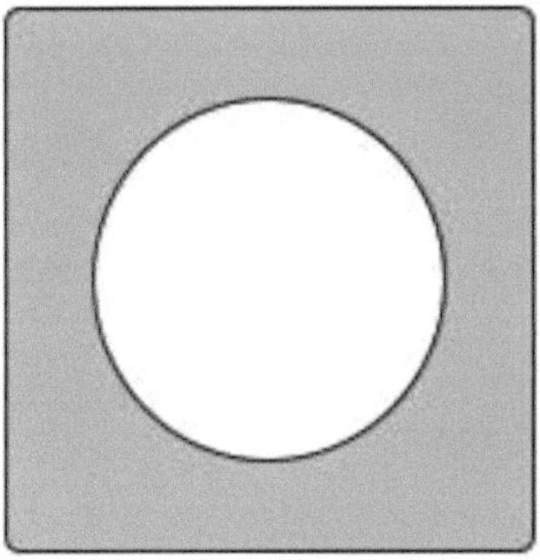

Figure 3.8: Figure/ground principle.

Figure 3.8: This illustration demonstrates the figure-ground principle of Gestalt psychology, which explains how humans perceive visual elements by distinguishing a primary object (figure) from its surrounding background (ground). In this image, the white circle appears as the figure because it draws attention and stands out prominently, while the surrounding gray square functions as the ground, receding into the background of our perception. This principle demonstrates how the visual system organizes scenes, enabling us to focus on specific elements while distinguishing them from less important surroundings.

The figure/ground principle is valuable in UX/UI design for more than creating visual interest. Designers use it to establish clear visual hierarchies and guide user attention. Modal windows illustrate this well: when a dialog box appears, the interface often darkens or blurs the background, allowing the modal to emerge as a distinct figure requiring immediate focus. Similarly, active form fields often increase in contrast with their surroundings, emphasizing their role as the current interactive focal point. These applications show how dynamic figure-ground relationships can shape user behavior and support task completion.

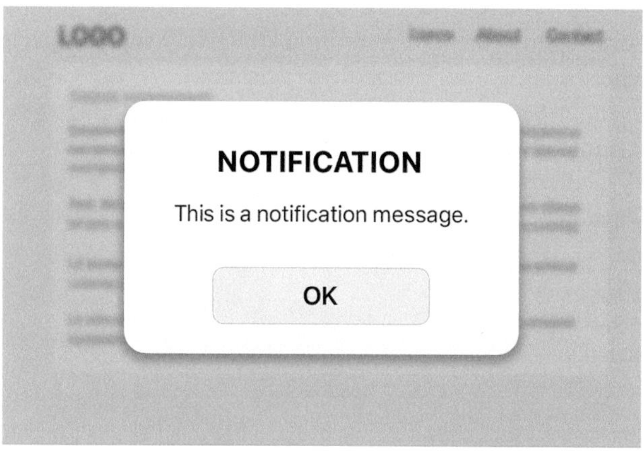

Figure 3.9: The white dialogue box serves as the figure, drawing focus as the primary element. The darkened surrounding screen functions as the ground, receding into the background to emphasize the message.

3.2.6 Symmetry & Order

The Law of Simplicity, commonly referred to as the Principle of Prägnanz or Good Figure, is a cornerstone of Gestalt psychology. It states that the human brain automatically simplifies complex or ambiguous visual information into the most straightforward and structured form. This propensity reduces cognitive load and supports efficient understanding of the world. Rather than perceiving fragmented or disorganized parts, the brain organizes them into recognizable, balanced, and cohesive forms.

The Olympic logo is an excellent example of Prägnanz. The overlapping rings are perceived as five distinct circles rather than a jumble of curved lines, even when displayed in a single color. This occurs because the brain favors symmetry and simplicity; it is easier to recognize complete circles than a complicated collection of broken arcs. The principle explains why human often perceive cohesive shapes even when some of their components are occluded or missing.

Figure 3.10: This illustration demonstrates the principle of symmetry and order, showing how the human brain organizes visual elements into balanced, structured forms for easier perception.

Prägnanz is powerfully illustrated by the way human interpret incomplete outlines. When partial outlines of triangles, circles, or rectangles appear in an image people instinctively "fill in the gaps" and perceive whole shapes rather than disconnected lines. This occurs because recognizing familiar, simple forms requires less mental effort than analyzing each line individually. Designers often apply this principle in logos, icons, and illustrations to help users recognize images more quickly and intuitively.

3.2.7 Additional Principles of Gestalt (Common Fate)

The principle of common fate, though not part of the original Gestalt principles, has emerged as an important concept in explaining human vision. It describes how elements moving in the same direction or sharing similar motion patterns are perceived as belonging together. In nature, for instance, a flock of birds flying in formation or a school of fish swimming in unison is automatically recognized as single, cohesive entity rather than as separate individuals. The brain clusters these moving elements because their shared motion implies they are part of a larger system. This perceptual tendency helps humans quickly interpret dynamic situations by reducing the cognitive effort required to analyze multiple moving parts individually.

The Figure 3.11 illustrates the Gestalt principle of Common Fate, a concept in visual perception. According to this principle, elements that move in the same

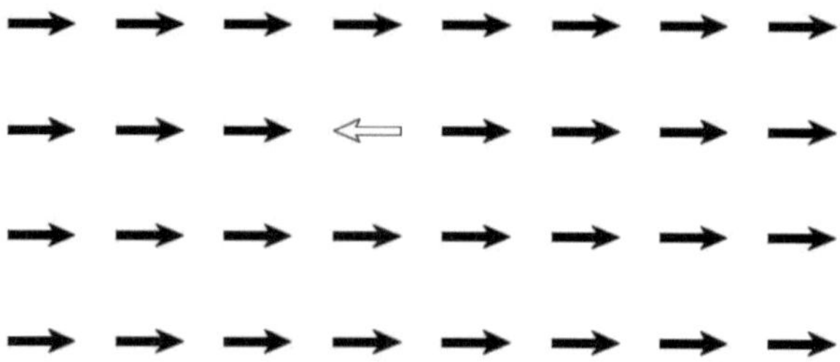

Figure 3.11: This illustration demonstrates the Gestalt principle of Common Fate, showing how elements moving in the same direction are perceived as part of the same group, while those moving differently stand out as separate.

direction or exhibit similar motion patterns are perceived as belonging to the same group. The brain links such elements together, interpreting their movement or orientation as evidence of a shared purpose or destination. In the second row, however, one arrow points to the left, opposite to the others. This arrow immediately stands out as separate from the group because its orientation breaks the common fate, making it visually distinct and perceived as an outlier.

The Common Fate principle has become increasingly important in user experience (UX) design, particularly as dynamic and animated interfaces have evolved. Designers use this principle to create interfaces that are intuitive and engaging, ensuring that related elements move, or appear to move, together. Examples include dropdown menus that expand smoothly, carousel slides that transition in sync, and progress indicators that animate sequentially. By animating elements in this way, designers can subtly indicate relationships between different areas of an interface, guide user attention, and enhance overall usability.

While Gestalt principles help users perceive the structure of an interface, the next set of principles, focused on decision-making, determine how easily they can navigate that structure, beginning with Hick's Law.

3.3 Hick's Law

Hick's Law states that the time required to make a decision increases with the number and complexity of available choices. Simplifying options and categorizing them effectively reduces cognitive load and improves decision-making efficiency. As shown in Figure 3.12, Google streamlines the search process by removing unnecessary content, allowing users to enter keywords quickly and without distractions.

Figure 3.13 illustrates Hick's Law, as the number of choices (x-axis) increases, response time (y-axis) also rises, demonstrating how decision-making

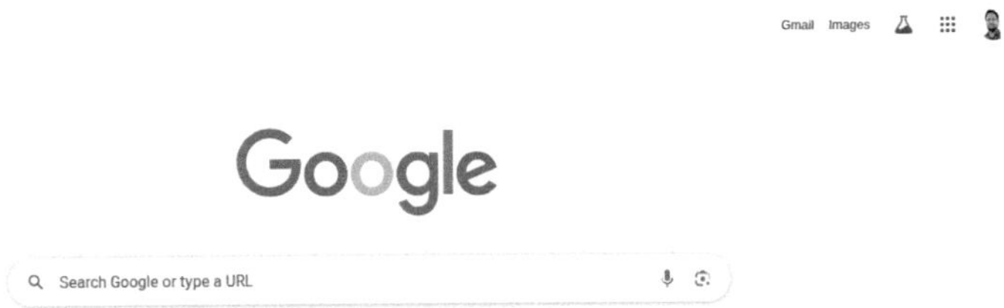

Figure 3.12: Google home page.

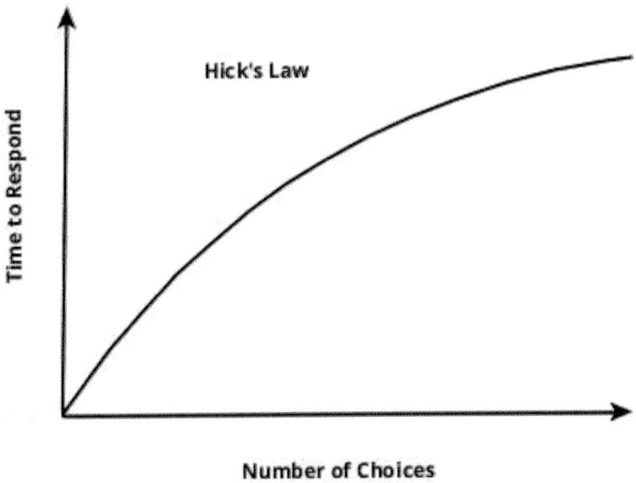

Figure 3.13: Hick's Law.

slows with more options. The upward trend, often logarithmic, shows that while adding a few choices has minimal impact, excessive options cause significant delays. This visual emphasizes why simplifying interfaces such as menus and dashboards enhances usability, aligning with design principles like K.I.S.S. to minimize cognitive overload and streamline user decisions. The K.I.S.S. concept ("Keep It Short and Simple") asserts that communications, designs, and systems function best when unnecessary complexity is eliminated. First introduced by the U.S. Navy and engineers in the 1960s, most notably in Kelly Johnson's aircraft designs, it supports Hick's Law by boosting productivity and reducing cognitive strain. By the 1970s, the principle had expanded into fields such as software, marketing, and product design, where simplicity improves usability and maintainability. In UX design, coding practices ("less is more"), and business strategies, K.I.S.S. remains fundamental today, demonstrating that clarity and conciseness often produce the best outcomes.

In psychology, Hick's Law, often referred to as the Hick–Hyman Law, explains how long it takes a person to make a decision based on the number of available options (Fitzgerald, A., 2023). Developed in the 1950s, by American psychologist Ray Hyman and British psychologist William Edmund Hick, the law can be expressed as:

$$RT = a + b.log_2(n) \tag{3.1}$$

where RT is the reaction time, a is the time not involved in decision-making, b is a constant representing the average time to process each piece of information, and n is the number of choices.

To illustrate Hick's Law, imagine designers creating a website navigation menu and assessing how the number of menu options impacts user decision time. Assume the following:

Baseline reaction time (a): 0.5 seconds

Additional time per bit of information (b): 0.2 seconds

For a menu with two options (e.g., "Home" and "Contact Us"), the decision time is short because users can quickly scan and select their choice. Applying Hick's Law:

$$RT = a + blog_2(N) = 0.5 + 0.2log_2(2) = 0.7seconds \tag{3.2}$$

With only two options (N = 2), the logarithmic term simplifies to 1, resulting in a reaction time of 0.7 seconds.

If the website contains four options, Home, About Us, Services, and Contact Us, the decision time increases, though not linearly. Users now have to consider four options, which means slightly more cognitive effort and time to make a choice. Then the reaction time is implemented using Hick's law as follows: $RT = 0.5 + 0.2log_2(4)$, which is equal to 0.9 seconds.

If the website contains eight options, Home, About Us, Services, Products, Blog, Careers, Contact Us, and Support—the decision time increases further. With eight options, users spend more time evaluating each choice. Applying Hick's Law: $RT = 0.5 + 0.2log_2(8)$, which is equal to 1.1 seconds.

3.3.1 Examples of Hick's Law

Some common examples of Hick's Law in action, both good and bad.

3.3.1.1 Website Design

Websites with 5–7 clear, well-organized main menu items are much faster to navigate than those with 15 or more crowded options. Users can process and select their choice more quickly. This is why mega-menus are popular on large e-commerce sites: they break down extensive choices into smaller, logical groups.

Flipkart demonstrates Hick's Law effectively by strategically managing its vast product range through categorization and curated options, as shown in Figure 3.14. The top navigation menu condenses millions of items into a few high-level categories, significantly reducing the user's initial decision load. This is reinforced by a prominent search bar for specific queries and highlighted promotional banners that serve as curated recommendations. Together, these design choices ensure users are not overwhelmed by too many simultaneous options and can make decisions quickly and confidently.

Figure 3.14: Home page of FlipKart.

3.3.1.2 Physical Product Design

A simple remote for a basic TV might have only 10 buttons (power, volume, channel, numbers). It is easy and fast to use. In contrast, a universal remote with 50+ small, identical buttons forces the user to slow down, scan carefully, and often make mistakes, an outcome directly explained by Hick's Law.

The Thomson remote image is a strong example of Hick's Law applied correctly. It features a limited number of distinct, well-spaced buttons (such as Power, VOL +/-, Channel +/-, and numbered keys) for primary functions. This small set of clear choices (n) enables users to make decisions and operate the TV quickly and almost instinctively, without being overwhelmed by complexity or forced to navigate a cluttered layout.

Figure 3.15: Thomson.

3.3.1.3 *Software & Application Design*

Microsoft Office transitioned from crowded toolbars (Office 2003) to the "Ribbon" interface (Office 2007 and later)[1]. The Ribbon groups related commands under tabs (Home, Insert, Design), effectively reducing the number of visible choices at any one time and making features easier to locate.

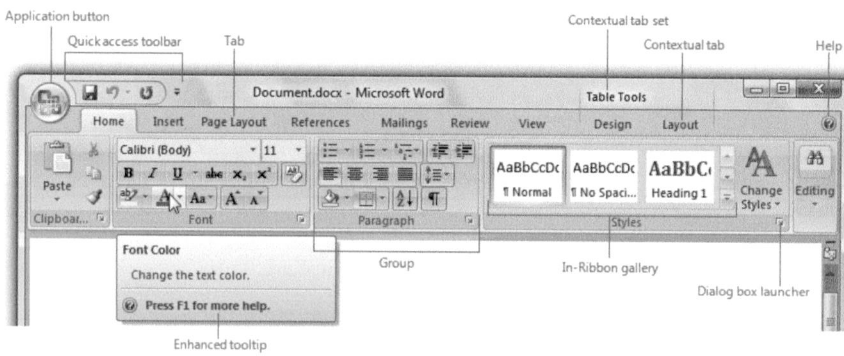

Figure 3.16: Microsoft office.

[1] https://learn.microsoft.com/en-us/windows/win32/uxguide/cmd-ribbons

3.4 Miller's Law

Miller's Law states that the average person can retain about seven (plus or minus two) items in working memory. According to Richard Greenan (2023), designers should limit the amount of information presented at one time to avoid overwhelming users. Miller proposed that working memory, the cognitive system responsible for temporarily holding and manipulating information, is limited to approximately seven items. This capacity can be expanded through grouping or "chunking" related pieces of information into single units. For example, a phone number such as "123-456-7890" consists of three chunks (area code, exchange, and number), making it easier to remember than a sequence of ten separate digits.

Designers and communicators can apply Miller's Law by presenting information in ways that respect the limitations of working memory. Breaking content into chunks or manageable groups helps users process and retain information more effectively. Some examples of Miller's law are as follows:

3.4.1 *Some Examples of Miller's Law*

The key to applying Miller's Law lies in understanding the concept of a "chunk." A chunk is a unit of information that is meaningful to the individual, it can be a single letter, a word, a phrase, or even a complex concept. Examples of Miller's Law can be observed across different fields:

3.4.1.1 User Interface (UI) & Website Design

Navigation Menus: Well-designed websites typically limit their main navigation items to around 5–7 options. More than this overwhelms users, making it difficult to process choices.

Amazon Homepage (Figure 3.17): Amazon applies Miller's Law strategically grouping its vast offerings into digestible units. For instance, the navigation bar consolidates numerous account features into high-level categories such as "Account & Lists" and "Returns & Orders," while the cart is presented as a distinct chunk. Similarly, a smartphone promotion is reduced to four key chunks—the product category ("Smartphones"), the price ("Starting 6,499"),

Figure 3.17: Amazon.

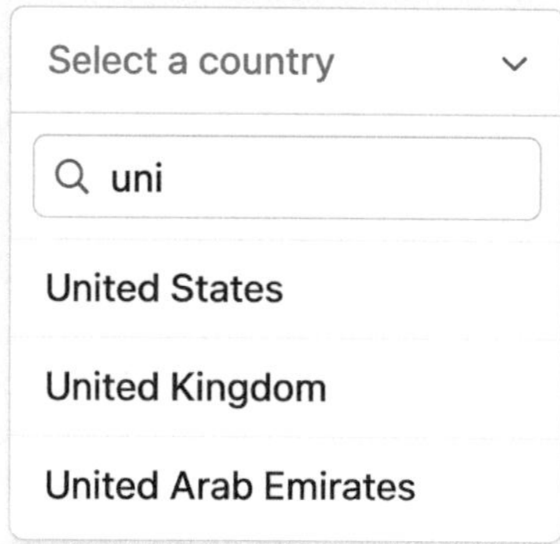

Figure 3.18: Example of dropdown.

and two financial benefits (No Cost EMI and Exchange Offer). This chunking presents a complex value proposition in a scannable format, preventing cognitive overload and enabling quick decision-making.

Forms & Dropdown Lists: Reducing the number of fields on a single form screen or limiting the options in a dropdown menu helps lower cognitive load. For instance, a nation-selection dropdown with approximately 195 selections violates Miller's Law. Users may attempt to chunk the list by typing "uni" to narrow it down to "United States," "United Kingdom," and similar entries. Designers counter this issue by adding a searchable text box at the top, as shown in Figure 3.18, allowing users to quickly filter and select their desired option.

3.4.1.2 Communication & Public Speaking

Effective speakers use Miller's Law to make their messages memorable through the "Rule of Three," a classic rhetorical technique in which information is presented in three main points. This structure fits comfortably within the limits of working memory. For over 15 years, Benjamin Ball (2024) and his associates have harnessed the power of the Rule of Three to transform business communication. By applying this principle, which emphasizes that ideas presented in threes are more memorable, persuasive, and complete, they refine speeches, investor pitches, and presentations, distilling complex messages into three clear, impactful points that resonate deeply with audiences and leave a lasting impression.

3.4.1.3 Everyday Life & Memory

- Phone Numbers: A ten-digit phone number like 1235557890 difficult to memorize as a string of ten separate digits because it exceeds our natural cognitive capacity. Humans overcome this by applying a familiar structure, chunking the number into three parts: (123) 555-7890. These chunks correspond to the area code, the prefix, and the line number. Instead of remembering ten individual items, people only need to hold three familiar, meaningful chunks in their minds. This principle is so effective that modern phones and user interfaces automatically format numbers in this way to reduce cognitive load and prevent errors.

- Chunking in Numerical and Financial Contexts: Humans also rely on chunking to interpret numerical and financial information efficiently. For example, a number like $49,999.00 is not read as a raw sequence of digits. Instead, perceptual cues such as commas and the decimal point break it into meaningful chunks. The commas segment the number by thousands, while the decimal separates the main amount from the cents. People then read it as a hierarchy of chunks: "forty-nine thousand", "nine hundred ninety-nine", and "dollars and zero cents". This process transforms a long string of digits into a logical, conceptual value that is easier to understand, compare, and remember, demonstrating how chunking is essential for navigating numerical data in everyday life.

3.4.1.4 Product Development & Marketing

Product Features: A large, disorganised list of product characteristics cause cognitive overload, making it difficult for customers to grasp the overall value proposition. For instance, a car with 50 new features becomes overwhelming concept if each is listed separately. Marketers address this by using chunking to group technical specifications into fewer, more comprehensive benefit categories. For example, functions such as lane-keep assist, blind-spot monitoring, and automatic emergency braking may be combined into a single package called the "Safety Suite."

Pricing Tiers: Chunking is equally important in guiding clients through complex pricing decisions. A Software-as-a-Service (SaaS) provider might theoretically offer a dozen individually priced features in countless combinations, but this would lead to "analysis paralysis", where consumers become so overwhelmed by options that they fail to make a decision at all. To counter this, organizations simplify the process by offering three or four pricing plans (e.g., Basic, Pro, and Business). Each plan is a pre-bundled set of features and costs tailored to a specific type of user. This reduces the vast array of choices into a clear, manageable comparison, making decision-making faster and more intuitive.

3.5 Jakob's Law

Users spend most of their time on other websites. As a result, they expect your site to function in ways consistent with the sites they already know. When designing a product, applying Jakob's law and aligning the design with the user's mental models reduces cognitive load. This means they don't need to invest extra time and energy learning how to use your product, which helps them feel at ease and makes the experience enjoyable. Jakob's Law was introduced by Jakob Nielsen, a user advocate and principal at the Nielsen Norman Group, which he co-founded with Dr. Donald A. Norman. According to Nielsen, J. (2023) the main drivers of Jakob's Law are:

- The first driver establishes the foundation of Jakob's Law: the vast array of digital options available to users. Because they spend limited time on any single site, users are unwilling to invest the mental effort required to master unique or unconventional interfaces. Given the economic realities of user attention, a design's success depends on minimizing cognitive burden. Any website that forces visitors to learn a new way to navigate, interact, or access information risks losing them to a more familiar competitor.

- The second driver explains how consumers navigate the overwhelming digital environment: they build mental models through chunking. Users do not consciously memorize every website they visit over time. Instead, they instinctively group common design patterns into recognizable categories. Elements such as the placement of a logo, the meaning of a shopping cart icon, and the structure of a navigation menu are learned in isolation on each site. Rather, they form part of a coherent mental image of "how a website works". These pre-formed chunks enable users to move through new sites quickly and efficiently.

- The third driver highlights the practical application of the learned mental model: it creates strong expectations. When users visit a new website, they do not begin from scratch; instead, they rely on their pre-chunked knowledge of established online norms. If a site aligns with these expectations, for example, placing the main navigation at the top or using blue, highlighted hyperlinks,the experience feels fluid and intuitive because users are drawing on familiar mental structures. Conversely, when a design disrupts these conventions, such as positioning the shopping cart in the bottom left corner, users must dismantle their efficient mental model and interpret the interface as a set of unfamiliar, disjointed elements. This leads to frustration, slower performance, and a greater likelihood of error.

3.5.1 Some Examples of Jakob's Law

A few examples illustrate that adhering to Jakob's Law represents the pinnacle of user-centric design and does not diminish creativity. Delivering a smooth, effective experience is a deliberate choice: it means communicating with users in a language they already understand, built from familiar fragments they have previously internalized.

3.5.1.1 The Principle of Predictable Placement (Search, Logo, Navigation)

The placement of search functionality, an open text box at the top-right of the page, is a clear example of chunking in navigation. Users have developed a mental model in which the "search chunk" occupies a specific location and appearance. By positioning it there, designers enable users to rely on their existing chunk rather than scanning the entire page to construct a new one. This same logic applies to the logo in the upper-left corner logo (chunked as "the button I click to go home") and the horizontal navigation bar at the top (chunked as "the main sections of this site"). These patterns are so deeply entrenched that disrupting them creates immediate friction and disorientation.

3.5.1.2 The Power of Universal Symbols (Shopping Cart Icon)

The shopping cart symbol is one of the most recognizable elements in the history of digital design. It exemplifies how a symbol can evolve beyond its literal meaning to become a universal mental model for "my selected items" and "proceed to purchase". Consumers do not perceive it as merely an icon; they see the function it represents in fulfilling their goal. Alternatives, such as a text link labeled "View Selections", require users to decode a new element rather than automatically recognizing a familiar one. This reliance on universal symbols is a cornerstone of intuitive e-commerce design.

3.5.1.3 Leveraging Inherited Platform Conventions (Scroll Bars, Pinch-to-Zoom)

These examples demonstrate that Jakob's Law extends beyond websites to the broader platforms, operating systems and mobile devices, on which sites and apps run. Through years of experience with iOS, Android, Windows, and macOS, users have learned simple interactions such as scrolling and zooming via years of experience with iOS, Android, Windows, and macOS. A website that employs the browser's native scroll bar leverages this prior understanding of how the widget works. Likewise, a mobile site that supports pinch-to-zoom draws on a gesture already embedded in users' mental model of "how to make something bigger." Departing from these platform-level chunks, for instance, by introducing a proprietary scrolling mechanism, almost always results in an interface that feels broken and difficult to use.

3.6 Fitts's Law

After users perceive an interface (Gestalt) and decide what action to take (Hick's, Miller's, Jakob's Law), they must physically execute that action. Fitts's Law models this physical interaction with precision. According to Raluca Budiu (2022), Fitts's Law states that the time required to acquire a target depends on both the distance to the target and its size. Larger buttons and clickable areas, especially those positioned near the user's focus of attention, enhance usability.

Paul Fitts was among the first psychologists to recognize that human error often arises from poor design rather than inherent human flaws. During World War II, he studied airplane cockpit layouts and argued that many incidents attributed to "pilot error" were actually the result of design deficiencies. In the 1950s, influenced by Shannon's famous information theory, Fitts sought to measure the bandwidth of human movement, much as George Miller applied the concept of channel capacity to memory when identifying the "magical number seven" as the limit of short-term recall. Through experiments on repetitive movements, Fitts formulated what became known as Fitts's Law, a foundational principle in human-computer interaction.

Fitts's Law describes the relationship between the time it takes a pointer (such as a mouse cursor, finger, or hand) to move to a target (e.g., a button or object) and interact with it (e.g., by clicking, tapping, or grasping):

$$T = a + b.log_2 \frac{2D}{w} \tag{3.3}$$

where D is the distance to the target, w is the width of the target (measured along the axis of movement), and a and b are constants that vary depending on the type of pointer (e.g., mouse, finger, etc.).

Consider a toolbar in a web application that includes several frequently used buttons (e.g., Save, Open). Designers aim to optimize the toolbar so users can quickly and accurately click these buttons. In this case, the Distance to the target (D) is 400 pixels, the Width of the target (W) is 50 pixels, Intercept (a) is 0.1 seconds (the base time to initiate and complete movement), and the Slope (b) is 0.2 seconds (the increase in time per unit of difficulty). Using Fitts's Law, the time can be calculated as follows: $T = 0.1 + 0.2.log_2 \frac{2*400}{50}$ which is equal to 0.9 seconds. Thus, the time required to move to the target is 0.9 seconds.

3.6.1 Application in User Interface Design

- Button Size: Larger buttons provide a bigger target area, reducing the precision required to click accurately. This lowers error rates (missed clicks) while increasing user speed and confidence.
- Proximity: Reducing the distance a user's cursor or finger must travel between related tasks significantly increases efficiency and establishes a logical flow. This principle is often referred to as the "Proximity Principle" in Gestalt psychology.
- Edge Advantage: One of the most ingenious applications of Fitts's Law is the use of screen edges and corners as infinitely large targets. Because the cursor cannot move beyond the screen boundary, users can "fling" their mouse toward a corner without fear of overshooting. This makes these locations exceptionally fast and easy to reach.

Fitts's Law has been widely applied in user interface design across websites and applications. Below are several examples of how its principles are integrated into web design:

3.6.1.1 Google Search

Google's search interface prominently features a large, centrally positioned search bar, making it easy for users to click and quickly enter their queries. The design reflects Fitts's Law by offering a sizeable, easily accessible target area that enhances speed and usability.

3.6.1.2 Windows Taskbar

The Windows Taskbar (or Dock in macOS) displays icons for frequently used applications and system functions. These icons are relatively large and positioned along the edge of the screen, making them easy to click. This design leverages Fitts's Law, which highlights the advantage of placing interactive elements at screen edges for faster and more accurate access.

3.6.1.3 Interface

Amazon's interface features numerous clickable elements, including product images, buttons, and links. These components are designed with appropriate sizes and spacing to support easy navigation and selection. By applying Fitts's Law, the design reduces the time and effort required for users to interact with the site, enhancing both efficiency and usability.

3.6.1.4 YouTube

YouTube's video player controls (play, pause, volume, etc.) are designed to be large and responsive, ensuring ease of use across different screen sizes and devices, as shown in Figure 3.19. The design allows users to interact with the controls quickly and accurately, reflecting Fitts's Law principles.

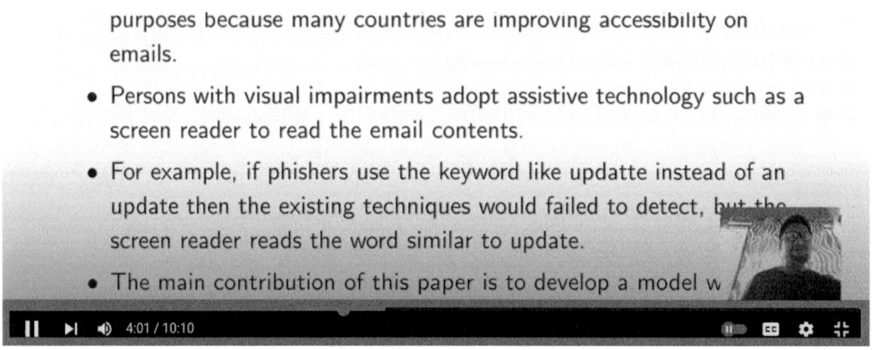

Figure 3.19: Youtube.

Beyond physical interaction, the Action & Motivation pillar also incorporates psychological drivers that foster engagement, such as the Von Restorff Effect.

3.7 Von Restorff Effect

The Von Restorff effect, also known as the isolation effect, states that when several similar objects are presented, the one that differs is more likely to be remembered. German psychologist Hedwig Von Restorff introduced the term in 1933. In her experiments, participants were shown lists in which one item stood out from the rest. She found that distinctive items were recalled more effectively than others, leading her to propose what is now known as the Von Restorff effect.

3.7.1 Some Examples of the Von Restorff Effect

According to Disha Mod. (2024), the findings of the Von Restorff effect findings are frequently applied in UX design to enhance user experience by strategically highlighting key elements within a digital interface.

Call-to-action buttons

This is a classic example of the Von Restorff effect. In an interface crowded with text, graphics, and links, the primary action button (e.g., "Buy Now," "Sign Up") is deliberately distinguished through: (1) Color: A striking, contrasting color that stands out from the site's core palette, (2) Size: Larger than secondary buttons or links to signal importance, (3) Whitespace: Adequate spacing to separate it from surrounding elements. These design choices ensure the button does not get lost in the visual noise. Instead, it immediately captures the user's attention and guides them toward the intended conversion goal without confusion.

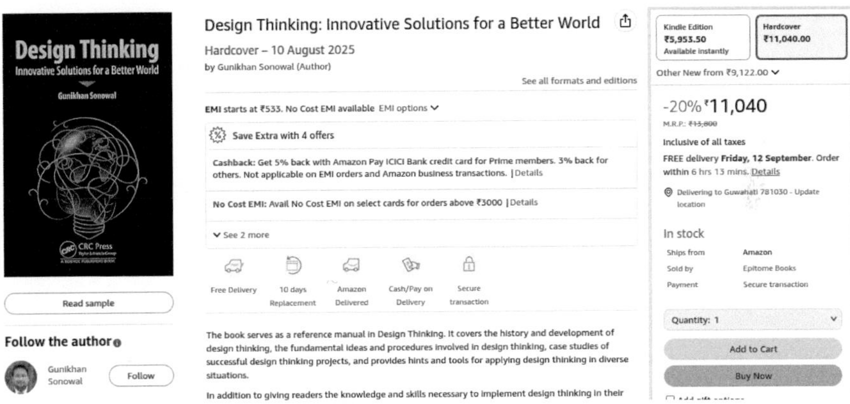

Figure 3.20: Amazon buy now button using Von Restorff effect.

Visual hierarchy

The Von Restorff effect is the psychological driver behind visual hierarchy. Hierarchy emerges when the most important elements are made distinct from less important ones. Designers apply the principle of isolation to signal priority: (1) Typography: A large, bold headline stands out from smaller body text. (2) Color: A brightly colored icon draws attention to a key feature. (3) Depth: A card with a drop shadow separates a special offer from the rest of the page. By manipulating attributes such as size, color, and contrast, designers establish a visual flow that directs the user's attention in order of importance, effectively reducing cognitive load.

Reduce cognitive load

This principle is applied by making key items, such as critical notifications or special offers, visually distinct through contrast in color, size, spacing, or animation. Doing so creates an immediate visual hierarchy that pre-processes information for the user, making it easier to interpret. Rather than canning and

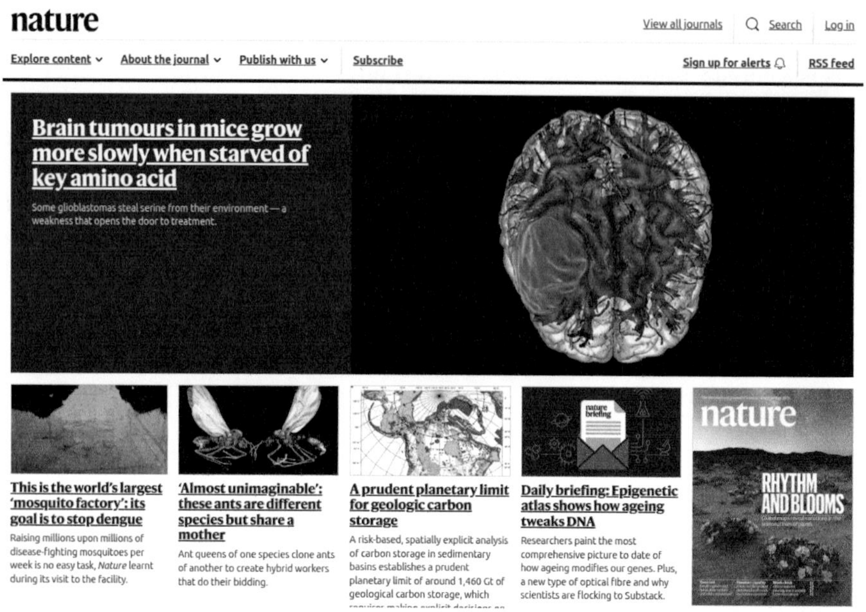

Figure 3.21: Nature homepage using visual hierarchy.

evaluating every element on a page to determine importance, users' attention is automatically drawn to the isolated element. This eliminates the need for conscious deduction, enabling users to quickly understand the interface and take action with minimal mental effort, resulting in a seamless and satisfying experience.

Brand identity

Brand identity leverages the Von Restorff effect to achieve memorability and differentiation. Companies such as Apple, Facebook, and Google employ unique logos, colors, and design elements to stand out in crowded marketplaces. Apple's half-bitten apple logo, Facebook's specific blue, and Google's multicoloured palette are intentionally isolated from competitors' branding. This distinctiveness not only enables instant recognition but also fosters emotional connections. When users encounter these distinctive elements elsewhere, they trigger brand recall, illustrating how the Von Restorff effect extends beyond interfaces into broader marketing and identity design.

Error handling

Effective error handling applies the Von Restorff effect to make problems unmistakable. Errors that blend into the interface (e.g., small, gray text) are easily overlooked, leading to user frustration. Instead, designers highlight errors through high-contrast colors (such as red text or borders), bold icons (like exclamation marks), and prominent placement. These techniques ensure that users immediately notice and address issues, reducing abandonment rates. For instance, a form field with an error might pulse red or display a bold message, making it the focal point until resolved. This approach prioritizes usability and prevents minor issues from derailing the user journey.

Form fields

Forms often suffer from high abandonment due to their repetitive and tedious nature. The Von Restorff effect helps counter this by introducing visual variety to sustain engagement. Designers may highlight active fields with a contrasting border color, apply distinct styles to differentiate required from optional fields, or make the submit button visually prominent. This techniques break the monotony of uniform text inputs and guide users through the process. For instance, a brightly colored "Submit" button at the end of a form serves as a clear finish line, encouraging completion while reducing perceived effort.

Progress indicators

Progress indicators apply the Von Restorff effect to reduce uncertainty in multi-step tasks. By visually distinguishing the current step (e.g., through color, bold text, or filled icons) from completed and upcoming steps, designers create a clear sense of movement and accomplishment. For instance, in a checkout process, the active step might appear in blue while others are gray, isolating the user's immediate task. This not only aids orientation but also motivates continuation by highlighting progress. Without such differentiation, users may feel lost or overwhelmed, increasing the likelihood of dropout.

3.8 Zeigarnik Effect

The Zeigarnik effect suggests that unfinished tasks are more memorable than completed ones. This phenomenon was first observed and described by Russian psychologist named Bluma Zeigarnik, a student of influential theorist Kurt Lewin. While sitting in a busy restaurant in Vienna, Ziegarnik noticed that waiters had better recall of unpaid orders. Once the bill was settled, however, they struggled to remember the exact details of those orders (Aguayo Publicidad, 2018).

The Zeigarnik Effect originated from a series of experiments conducted by Bluma Zeigarnik in which participants were asked to perform multiple tasks, some completed, others left unfinished. Zeigarnik observed that participants more easily remembered incomplete tasks than completed ones. She concluded that the human mind actively retains pending tasks, creating a sense of mental tension until they are resolved.

The mechanism behind the Zeigarnik Effect relates to how the brain processes and stores information. When a task is incomplete, the brain keeps it active in working memory, increasing the likelihood of recall and eventual completion. This "cognitive load" associated with incomplete tasks drives individuals to focus their attention on them until they are finished.

The Zeigarnik Effect has several practical applications in everyday life as well as in fields such as marketing, advertising, and user experience (UX) design. For instance, in product and application design, strategies can be employed to keep users engaged and motivated by presenting incomplete tasks or goals.

Applications of the Zeigarnik Effect in User Experience: Discovered by Russian psychologist Bluma Zeigarnik in the 1920s, the Zeigarnik Effect has been widely applied in UX design. This psychological phenomenon, highlighting the mind's tendency to remember and focus on unfinished tasks, offers valuable insights for creating effective and engaging digital interfaces.

3.8.1 Application of Zeigarnik Effect

The Zeigarnik Effect is a psychological principle stating that people remember unfinished or interrupted tasks better than completed ones. This phenomenon occurs because the mind experiences a state of cognitive tension, a kind of mental itch, when a task is left incomplete. That tension keeps the task at the forefront of memory, creating an urge to return to it and achieve closure, thereby relieving the psychological discomfort.

3.8.1.1 Productivity and Procrastination

In the realm of personal productivity, the Zeigarnik Effect serves as a powerful tool against procrastination. It explains why the simple act of starting a task, even in a small way, creates a mental pull to finish it. Techniques such as making a to-do list leverage this effect by externalizing tasks and creating a series of unfinished items that the brain feels compelled to complete. Additionally, intentionally pausing work on a complex project at a point where the next step is clear makes it significantly easier to resume later, as the unresolved tension draws us back to the task.

3.8.1.2 Marketing and Advertising

Marketers and advertisers skillfully apply the Zeigarnik Effect to capture attention and drive consumer engagement. They create open loops through multi-part campaigns, cliffhanger endings in commercials, and serialized content that audiences feel compelled to follow to completion. Progress bars in apps and websites gamify the user experience, sparking the desire to finish an activity or profile to reach 100%. The same principle underlies the "free trial" model, where interrupted access generates an urge to pay for the full, completed service.

3.8.1.3 Learning and Education

The Zeigarnik Effect offers significant benefits for learning and knowledge retention. Students can harness it by ending a study session not at the close of a chapter, but in the middle of a problem or an engaging section. This interruption makes the material more memorable and creates a natural pull to resume studying later. Educators apply the same principle by posing a compelling question at the start of a lecture and delaying the answer, keeping students engaged and attentive as their minds seek resolution.

3.8.1.4 Storytelling and Media

The world of storytelling is perhaps the most classic domain of the Zeigarnik Effect. Television series, book series, and podcasts often employ cliffhangers at the end of an episode or chapter. By interrupting the narrative at a moment of high tension, they create an unresolved loop in the viewer's or reader's mind. This powerful sense of anticipation ensures the audience returns for the next installment to gain closure and relieve the cognitive tension generated by the unfinished story.

3.8.2 Negative Implications and Management

However, if left unmanaged, the Zeigarnik Effect can have negative consequences. A constant stream of unfinished tasks can lead to stress, anxiety, and mental clutter, as the brain remains preoccupied with unresolved loops. To mitigate this, it is essential to manage the effect by recording tasks in a trusted system, signaling to the brain that the task has been captured and can be released from immediate memory. Effective planning and prioritization further help transform overwhelming cognitive tension into a structured, manageable action plan.

3.9 Conclusion

Understanding the psychology of user behavior is essential for effective UI/UX design. The tripartite framework of Perception, Decision-Making, and Action & Motivation provides a systematic approach to this understanding. By applying principles within this framework, from Gestalt's organization of visual information to the motivational pull of the Zeigarnik Effect, designers can craft interfaces that are not only intuitive and efficient but also deeply engaging. Ultimately, aligning design with the fundamental ways users see, think, and act is the key to creating products that truly meet user needs and deliver a compelling experience.

Chapter 4

Information Architecture

Information Architecture (IA) forms the strategic backbone of User Experience (UX) design, translating user needs and business objectives into a structural blueprint for digital products. By deliberately organizing, structuring, and labeling content, IA reduces cognitive load and creates intuitive pathways for navigation and discovery. Grounded in the principles of cognitive psychology, IA seeks aligns information systems with users' mental models, ensuring logical and predictable structures. This enhances usability, empowers users to locate information efficiently, and enables task completion with minimal friction. Ultimately, effective information architecture is not merely a preliminary step but a critical determinant of a product's overall success and user satisfaction.

4.1 Definition and Importance of IA

The concept of Information Architecture (IA) has evolved over time, with different authors emphasizing various components of the field. Below is an overview of definitions from prominent thought leaders.

The information design approach is fundamentally rooted in Richard Saul Wurman's original vision. For Wurman, architecture and design provided the foundation for a discipline dedicated to creating "instructions for organized space" and, crucially, for rendering that space understandable. The concept of understanding is central to his work; his objective was always to make the complex clear (Resmini & Rosati, 2012).

This mission was crystallized in his seminal 1997 book Information Architects, published just one year before Rosenfeld and Morville's Information Architecture for the World Wide Web. Wurman's book was a direct response

DOI: 10.1201/9781003715764-4

to what he identified as growing "information anxiety", the difficulty of communicating and processing ever-increasing amounts of data. Rather than a technical manual, it was a designer's book: a curated collection of visual and structural solutions to this problem, created by a designer for designers. Wurman defined information architecture as:

- An individual who organizes the patterns inherent in data, making the complex clear;
- A person who creates the structure or map of information that allows others to find their personal paths to knowledge;
- An emerging 21st-century professional occupation addressing the needs of an age focused on clarity, human understanding, and the science of organizing information (Wurman, 1989).

Wurman maintained a strong analogy to physical architecture. He argued that just as architects impose structure and order on the physical world through planning and building, information architects must draw boundaries and establish order within the dataspace. Their primary task, therefore, is not merely to organize but to simplify, clarify, and make information comprehensible.

In their book Information Architecture for the World Wide Web (1998), Rosenfeld et al., established IA as a critical discipline for the web. Known as the "Polar Bear Bible," the book remains one of the most widely cited sources in UX (Rosenfeld et al., 2015). They defined information architecture as the structural design of shared information environments, serving as the foundational framework that organizes these spaces. It represents the synthesis of organization, labeling, search, and navigation systems across digital, physical, and cross-channel ecosystems. As both an art and a science, IA is dedicated to shaping information products and experiences that support usability, findability, and effective understanding. Over time, this practice has emerged as a vital discipline and community, applying the enduring principles of design and architecture to the complexities of the modern digital landscape.

In the Elements of User Experience (Garrett, 2002) presented a model that positioned Information Architecture (IA) within a broader UX framework. Garrett defined IA as fundamentally concerned with the structural design of information spaces. Drawing a direct parallel to the work of physical architects, information architects must first deeply understand user needs in order to design structures that facilitate the derivation of meaning and knowledge. These structures manifest not only in the digital realm, such as websites and applications, but also in the physical world through objects like maps, signage, and built environments. A comprehensive view of these spaces also includes the people within them, who act both as consumers and generators of content, continuously shaping the ecosystem. Because structuring information is a foundational pillar of user experience, a UX designer must, at various points in the design process, effectively assume the role of an information architect.

Information architecture is thus the deliberate practice of structuring and organizing information environments to be intuitive, manageable, and meaningful, enabling users to locate information and complete tasks with minimal friction.

4.2 Components of Information Architecture

According to (Morville & Rosenfeld, 2006), four key components of information architecture are shown in Table 4.1. This framework provides a concise way to understand the core elements that constitute an information architecture. Organizational Systems address how information is categorized and structured, employing hierarchies, taxonomies, and classification schemes to create a logical backbone. Labeling Systems meet the critical need for clear communication by defining what information is called, using consistent navigation labels, headings, and links that speak the user's language. Navigation Systems explain how users move through the information environment, offering wayfinding tools like global menus, local menus, and breadcrumbs to support exploration and browsing. Search Systems serve users looking for something specific, encompassing everything from the query box and underlying algorithms to the filters and results displays that enable direct retrieval. Together, these four systems form an interdependent framework that allows users not only to find what they need but also to understand what they find.

Table 4.1: The four core components of information architecture.

Component	Core Question it Answers	Key Elements
Organizational Systems	How is the information categorized and structured?	Hierarchies, taxonomies, facets, organization schemes (exact/ambiguous), database structures
Labeling Systems	What is this called?	Navigation labels, headings, contextual links, index terms, iconic labels
Navigation Systems	How do I move through the information?	Global navigation, local navigation, contextual navigation, breadcrumbs, sitemaps, indexes
Search Systems	How do I find something specific?	Query box, search algorithms, filters, facets, results display, query builders

4.2.1 Organizational Systems

Organizational systems form the foundational layer of information architecture, creating the logical framework that determines how content is categorized and interrelated. The primary purpose of organization is pragmatic: to help users locate information efficiently while developing a coherent understanding of the information environment. This requires supporting two distinct but equally important user behaviors:

- **Directed Searching:** When users know precisely what they are looking for and need to find it quickly.
- **Casual Browsing:** When users explore with undefined or evolving information needs, discovering content through serendipitous navigation.

Despite the technical flexibility of digital media to support virtually any organizational scheme, this very freedom often leads to poorly conceived, confusing systems. This paradox underscores the fundamental challenges inherent in structuring information effectively.

4.2.1.1 Challenges in Organizing Information

Creating effective organizational systems requires navigating four persistent challenges:

- **Ambiguity:** Natural language is inherently imprecise. Words often carry multiple meanings (for example, "pitch" in sports, music, or business), and content may legitimately belong to multiple categories. This linguistic flexibility makes it difficult to create mutually exclusive categories.
- **Heterogeneity:** Unlike homogeneous collections like library card catalogs, digital environments contain diverse content types, formats, and levels of granularity, from PDF reports and product videos to employee profiles and interactive tools. No single organizational structure can optimally accommodate such varied content.
- **Differences in Perspective:** Individuals organize information based on unique mental models shaped by their background, expertise, and goals. A categorization system that seems perfectly logical to a technical expert may be incomprehensible to a novice user. Overcoming this requires extensive user research to identify and design for common mental models.
- **Internal Politics:** Organizational decisions are rarely purely objective. Determining which content receives prominent placement or specific labels often becomes politically charged, involving negotiations among

departments, stakeholders, and competing priorities. Successful information architects must navigate these dynamics while maintaining user-centered design principles.

4.2.1.2 *Organization Schemes*

Organizational systems comprise both *schemes* (the criteria for grouping items) and *structures* (the relationships between groups). Organization schemes fall into two primary categories:

Exact Organization Schemes

These objective, unambiguous schemes use consistent, pre-defined criteria that yield mutually exclusive categories. They are especially effective for supporting directed searching, when users know precisely what they are looking for.

- **Alphabetical:** Ideal for directories, indexes, and glossaries (e.g., employee A-Z listings, dictionary entries).
- **Chronological:** Effective for time-sensitive content like news archives, event calendars, and version histories.
- **Geographical:** Essential for location-based information, particularly in mobile and mapping applications.

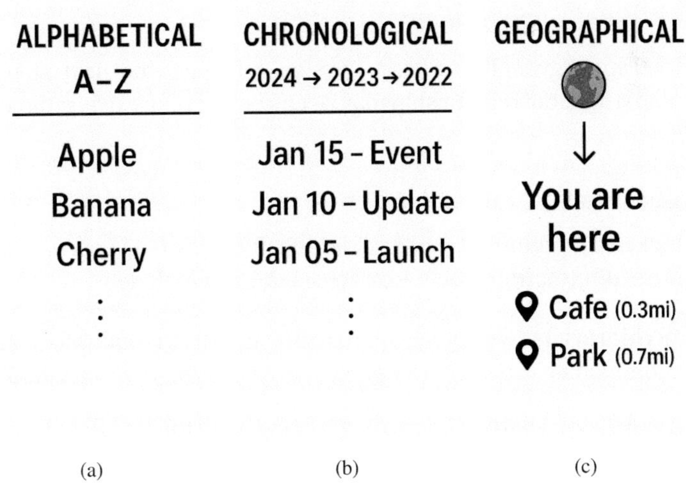

Figure 4.1: (a) Alphabetical, (b) Chronological, (c) Geographical.

Ambiguous Organization Schemes

These subjective, intellectually-derived schemes group content based on meaning and context rather than objective rules. They are crucial for supporting browsing and discovery.

- **Topical:** Organizes content by subject matter (e.g., "Product Reviews," "Industry News"). This is one of the most common and intuitive schemes.
- **Task-Oriented:** Groups content by user actions and processes (e.g., "Download Software," "Contact Support").
- **Audience-Specific:** Tailors content to particular user groups (e.g., "For Students," "For Developers"). While effective for personalization, this approach risks fragmenting content for users who belong to multiple audiences.
- **Metaphor-Driven:** Leveraging familiar real-world concepts (e.g., "shopping cart," "digital library") can ease the learning curve by helping users quickly understand digital interactions. However, metaphors may become limiting if stretched beyond their natural boundaries, potentially confusing users or constraining design flexibility.
- **Hybrid Schemes:** Thoughtfully combining multiple schemes can address diverse user needs, however, complex hybrids risk creating cognitive dissonance if not carefully implemented.

4.2.1.3 Organization Structures

After establishing grouping criteria through schemes, the next step involves defining the structural relationships between these groups using three primary models.

Hierarchical Structure (Top-Down)

The familiar tree structure of parent-child relationships helps users form mental models of the information space. Key considerations include:

- **Polyhierarchy:** Allowing content to appear in multiple locations to accommodate different user perspectives and improve findability.
- **Breadth vs. Depth Balance:** Avoiding structures that are too shallow (overwhelming users with options) or too deep (forcing excessive clicking). The optimal balance depends on content complexity and user goals.

Database Structure (Bottom-Up)

This model treats content as structured records with defined metadata fields, enabling powerful, dynamic organization:

- Field-specific searching and filtering (by author, date, category, etc.)
- Sophisticated sorting and relational linking between content items
- Ideal for homogeneous content collections like product catalogs, employee directories, and CMS-managed content

Hypertext Structure

Hypertext enables non-linear, associative linking between content items, mimicking human thought processes. While offering maximum flexibility, it can disorient users if overused and is best employed to complement, rather than replace, hierarchical and database structures.

4.2.1.4 Social Classification

The rise of social media has introduced user-driven organization through tagging systems that create "folksonomies", emergent, organic categorization systems. While not replacing formal taxonomies, social classification provides valuable supplemental organization through:

- **Social Navigation:** Discovering content through collective behavior patterns (e.g., trending hashtags).
- **Vocabulary Capture:** Documenting the natural language and terminology of user communities.
- **Flexible Organization:** Adding a dynamic, bottom-up layer to complement top-down taxonomic structures.

4.2.1.5 Synthesis: A Pragmatic Approach

Effective organizational systems typically employ a mixed-methods approach, acknowledging that no single solution is perfect. The most successful implementations:

- Combine exact and ambiguous schemes to support both searching and browsing behaviors.
- Use hierarchical structures for the overall framework while leveraging database models for structured content and hypertext for associative connections.

- Decompose complex sites into manageable, more homogeneous subsections.
- Focus on creating systems that feel intuitive to users, even if the underlying architecture is complex.

The ultimate goal is not theoretical purity but practical effectiveness, designing organizational systems that feel natural to users while efficiently supporting their information-seeking activities.

4.2.2 Labeling Systems

Labeling systems serve as the communicative layer of information architecture, translating complex information structures into understandable user interfaces. A label functions as a representational shortcut, whether textual or graphical, that stands in for a broader, more complex set of information. The primary objectives of labeling are to convey meaning efficiently while conserving both valuable screen real estate and, more importantly, the user's cognitive resources. Although labeling is a fundamental human activity that often occurs unconsciously, neglecting deliberate attention to labeling decisions frequently results in confusing website terminology. Labels act as the critical connective tissue linking organizational structures and navigation systems to the end user, making intentional label design essential during implementation.

4.2.2.1 The Critical Role of Labeling

The importance of precise labeling becomes particularly acute in digital environments, where immediate feedback mechanisms are absent. Unlike face-to-face communication, where misunderstandings can be quickly resolved through visual cues and dialogue, digital interfaces require labels that are self-explanatory at first encounter. A practical way to evaluate labeling effectiveness is to examine a website's prominent labels in isolation from its visual design, assessing each for clarity, necessity, and likely user interpretation.

This approach was demonstrated through a Starbucks website case study, which identified several problematic labels: the ambiguous "Menu" (does it display food items or navigation options?), the internally-focused "Coffeehouse" (meaningless to many customers), and the overly broad "Card" (referring to gift cards, loyalty cards, or payment methods?). The analysis revealed that poor labeling leads to multiple negative outcomes, including failure to accurately represent content, reliance on internal jargon rather than user-centric language, financial losses due to user abandonment, and damage to brand perception. These findings position effective labeling as equally critical to success as visual design or content quality.

4.2.2.2 *Types of Labels in Digital Environments*

Labeling systems encompass several distinct types, each serving specific functions within the information architecture:

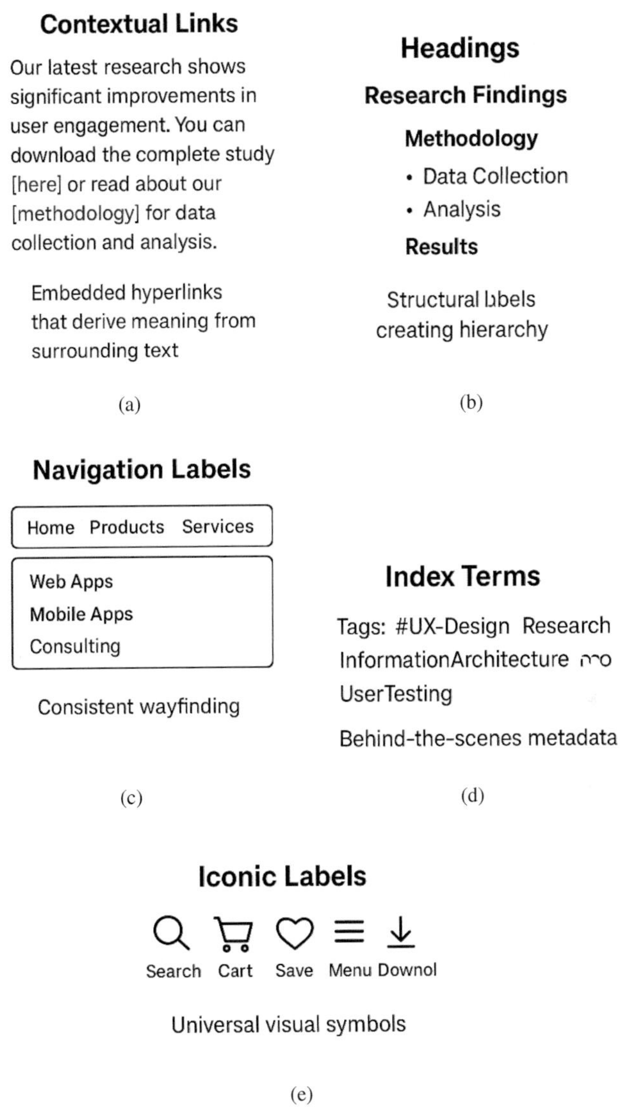

Figure 4.2: (a) Contextual labeling, (b) Heading labeling, (c) Navigation labeling, (d) Index labeling, (e) Iconic labeling.

- **Contextual Links:** Hyperlinks embedded within body content that derive meaning from their surrounding text. Their effectiveness depends heavily on the author's ability to create meaningful anchor text that accurately predicts the destination content.
- **Headings:** Labels that describe subsequent content sections while establishing a visual hierarchy. Well-structured headings can compensate for minor wording imperfections through their clear structural relationships.
- **Navigation Labels:** Options within global and local menus that demand the highest level of consistency. As the primary wayfinding mechanism repeated across the entire site, inconsistent navigation labels disrupt user mental models and erode trust.
- **Index Terms:** Keywords, tags, and metadata that describe content for search and retrieval systems. These behind-the-scenes labels power search functionality and faceted browsing interfaces.
- **Iconic Labels:** Visual representations that conserve space and enhance aesthetics. Given their inherent ambiguity, iconic labels work best for small sets of universally recognized actions (e.g., shopping cart, search magnifying glass, menu hamburger).

4.2.2.3 Designing Effective Labeling Systems

Creating effective labels balances art and science, navigating the inherent ambiguity of natural language while establishing systematic consistency. Key principles include:

- **Scope Definition:** Narrowing content scope to simplify labeling tasks and improve precision.
- **Systemic Consistency:** Developing consistent labeling systems rather than merely consistent individual labels, maintaining uniformity across style, presentation, syntax, and granularity.
- **Source Integration:** Drawing label inspiration from multiple sources, including current content audits, competitive analysis, existing controlled vocabularies, and most importantly, direct user input through methods like card sorting and search-log analysis.

The most reliable source of effective labels comes from users, either through research methods such as free-listing exercises or indirectly by analyzing search query logs that reveal their natural language and terminology preferences.

4.2.2.4 Maintenance and Evolution of Labeling Systems

Labeling systems require ongoing refinement to remain effective over time. The maintenance process involves:

- **Systematic Organization:** Sorting, deduplicating, and standardizing labels according to established style conventions.
- **Comprehensiveness Audit:** Identifying and addressing content gaps while avoiding vague "catch-all" categories that reduce findability.
- **Scope Management:** Balancing comprehensive coverage against maintainability to prevent system bloat.
- **Continuous Improvement:** Establishing processes for regular label refinement based on usability testing, search analytics, and user feedback to accommodate evolving language and content.

Labeling represents a foundational yet often underestimated component of information architecture. The most effective labels operate invisibly, seamlessly connecting users to content without drawing attention to themselves. They bridge the gap between the system's structure and the user's mental model. While labeling remains an art form that must navigate linguistic ambiguity, a disciplined approach, grounded in user research, committed to systemic consistency, and dedicated to continuous refinement, enables the creation of labeling systems that form the backbone of successful user experiences.

4.2.3 Navigation Systems

Much like the disorientation felt in an unfamiliar city, users experience frustration and cognitive strain when lost within poorly designed digital environments. Throughout history, humans have developed sophisticated wayfinding tools, from physical breadcrumbs to modern GPS, to navigate complex spaces. In digital contexts, while not life-threatening, effective navigation remains crucial for preventing user confusion and task abandonment. A powerful architectural metaphor illustrates this relationship: if organizational systems construct the rooms of a digital house, then navigation systems install the doors, windows, and hallways that enable movement and exploration.

4.2.3.1 The Nature of Digital Navigation

This section focuses specifically on navigation systems designed for *browsing*, the process of exploring and discovering content through intentional movement. While treated separately from search systems, both browsing and searching together form complementary components of a comprehensive findability strategy that also includes structural organization and labeling. Contemporary navigation design must also account for the evolving landscape of responsive design, where navigation patterns adapt significantly across devices and screen sizes, from expansive desktop layouts to thumb-friendly mobile interfaces.

4.2.3.2 Primary Navigation System Categories

Navigation systems fall into two fundamental categories based on their integration with primary content:

Embedded Navigation Systems

These systems are woven directly into the fabric of each page, providing constant wayfinding support:

- **Global Navigation:** The persistent navigation bar, typically positioned at the top or side of every page, offers consistent access to key site areas. Modern implementations face critical design trade-offs between simplicity and information density. Advanced patterns such as *mega-menus* (offering rich content previews) and *fat footers* (serving as condensed site maps) have emerged as effective solutions for complex information environments.
- **Local Navigation:** This system enables exploration within specific site sections or subsites. Local navigation may be tightly integrated with global navigation (creating a seamless hierarchy) or operate as distinct sub-environment with unique navigation schemes, often reflecting decentralized content ownership or specialized user needs.
- **Contextual Navigation:** Comprising "See Also," "Related Articles," or "People Also Bought" links, contextual navigation creates associative connections between content items outside the primary hierarchy. These links support serendipitous discovery, cross-content relationships, and associative learning by revealing connections users might not otherwise discover.

The simultaneous implementation of all three embedded systems presents ongoing design challenges, particularly regarding screen real estate allocation and visual hierarchy. Design decisions regarding text-versus-icon representation and placement conventions vary significantly between desktop (with ample space) and mobile contexts (where navigation is often collapsed or repositioned for ergonomic accessibility).

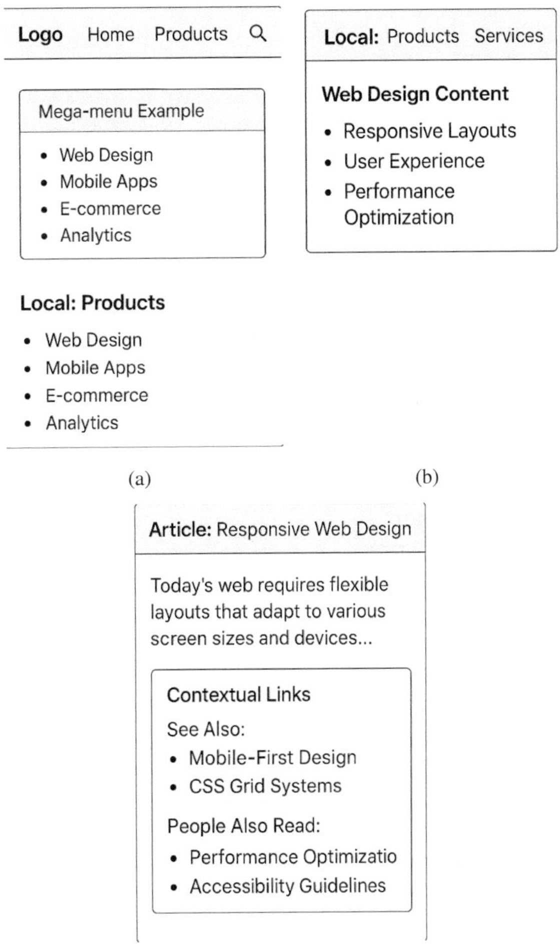

(c)

Figure 4.3: (a) Global navigation provides persistent access to key site areas with mega-menu previews, (b) local navigation enables section-specific exploration within content hierarchies, (c) Contextual navigation creates associative connections between related content items for serendipitous discovery.

Supplemental Navigation Systems

These secondary systems provide alternative access points when primary navigation fails or when users require different wayfinding approaches:

- **Sitemaps:** Offering a bird's-eye hierarchical view, sitemaps reinforce the overall information architecture while enabling random access to major content areas.

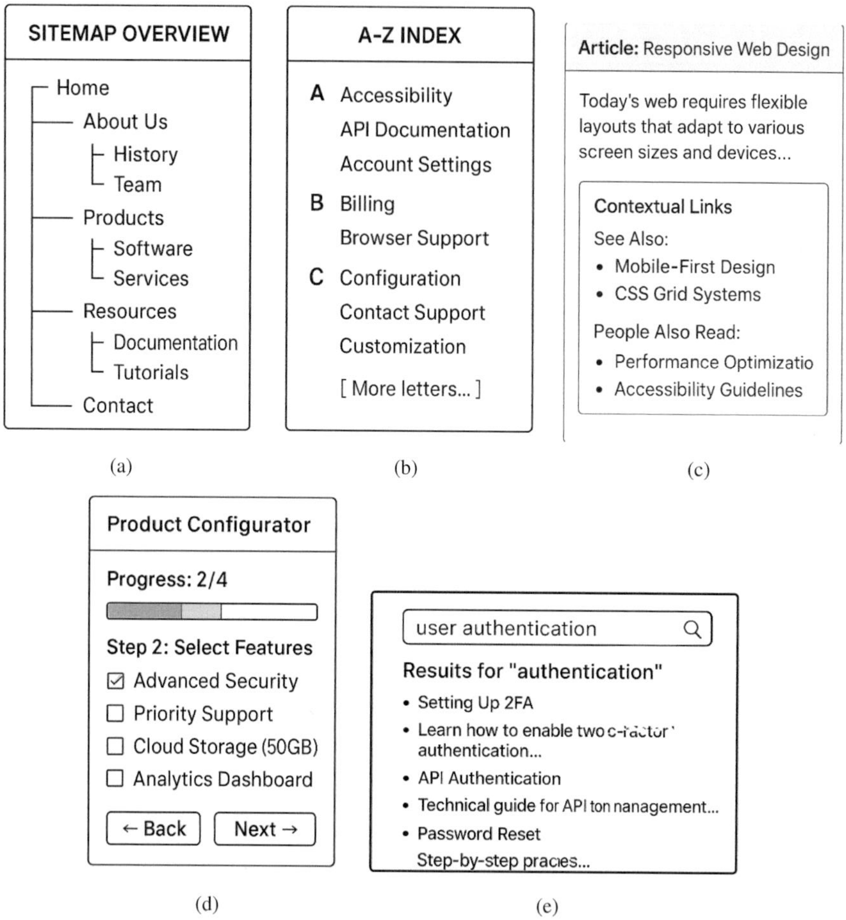

Figure 4.4: Supplemental navigation systems: (a) Sitemap, (b) Index, (c) Guide, (d) Configurators, (e) Search.

- **Indexes:** As alphabetical keyword lists, indexes bypass hierarchical structures entirely, making them ideal for known-item searching when users recall specific terms but not their structural location.
- **Guides:** Tutorial-style pathways that orient new users or walk them through complex processes, often combining instructional narrative with interface demonstrations.
- **Configurators:** A specialized guide variant, configurators (or wizards) assist users through multi-step decision processes, such as product customization, by providing clear feedback and progress indicators.

- **Search:** While deserving its own comprehensive treatment, search functions as a critical supplemental navigation tool, operating in tandem with browsing systems.

4.2.3.3 Advanced Navigation Paradigms

Beyond fundamental systems, several sophisticated navigation approaches address specific user needs and contexts:

Personalization and Customization

- **Personalization:** System-driven adaptation of navigation based on user behavior, preferences, and history. Effective implementation requires robust user tracking and algorithmic sophistication.

- **Customization:** User-controlled modification of navigation elements. Both approaches demand solid structural foundations and typically see highest utilization on frequently-visited sites where user investment justifies the complexity.

Visual Navigation

Visual interfaces become particularly valuable when appearance drives selection criteria, for example, in e-commerce product browsing, interior design applications, or fashion retail, where visual characteristics are the primary decision factors.

Social Navigation

This emerging paradigm filters and prioritizes navigation options based on collective user behavior and social connections. As demonstrated on platforms like Reddit and Facebook, social navigation leverages crowd wisdom but requires careful design to avoid creating "filter bubbles" and echo chambers that restrict exposure to diverse perspectives.

4.2.3.4 Synthesis: Cohesive Navigation Strategy

Effective navigation design ultimately depends on maintaining consistent global structures that establish reliable mental models, while incorporating supplemental and advanced systems to address diverse user needs and contexts. The most successful navigation ecosystems balance predictable wayfinding with flexible access methods, ensuring that users can always determine their location, navigate efficiently to desired destinations, and discover relevant content they may not have known to seek.

4.2.4 Search Systems

A search system provides users a direct route to content, enabling them to bypass navigation and quickly locate what they need, whereas browsing systems offer a more organized, exploratory approach. Strategic search design goes far beyond simply "adding a search box." It involves analyzing the situations in which search is truly required, examining how users articulate their needs, and developing a framework for user interfaces and indexing techniques that transform search from a blunt instrument into a precise tool for discovery.

4.2.4.1 The Strategic Case for Site Search

The decision to develop a search system is critical, not incidental. It must be driven by user needs and content architecture, not tradition. A poorly designed search tool can be more damaging than its absence, creating noise, frustration, and the impression of a disorganised site.

Search is often misused as a cosmetic workaround for fundamental information architecture flaws. If users struggle to navigate a site, adding a search engine to an already broken layout only compounds the confusion. The first priority is to ensure that the browsing system is logical; search should supplement, not replace, a strong foundation. Moreover, for small, tightly structured sites with limited content, a comprehensive search index may be unnecessary, adding maintenance complexity without delivering proportional user benefit.

Search evolves from a feature into a necessity under two conditions: the scale of the content and the rate at which it changes. As a site grows organically, like a bookshop extending into neighbouring shopfronts, the cognitive load of viewing its full structure becomes overwhelming. Users with specific intentions will expect a direct route. Similarly, for content-driven sites with a high levels of dynamism, such as news portals, blogs, or product catalogues, search is the only scalable mechanism for ensuring that new information is immediately accessible without requiring constant manual curation of navigation menus.

4.2.4.2 The User's Search Mindset: Beyond the Query Box

A query is only the visible outcome of a user's specific information need, cognitive process, and level of skill. When designing an efficient search system, it is essential to recognize the diverse range of information requirements, as user searches are rarely consistent. Common search intentions include:

1. Known-Item Search: The user has a defined target, such as a product model number or a particular contact. Success is binary, they either find the exact item or fail.

2. Exploratory Search: The user investigates a subject without a precise objective (e.g., "options for home solar power"). The focus is on learning, comparison, and understanding breadth rather than depth.

3. Comprehensive Research: The user seeks thoroughness, aiming to compile all relevant data on a subject for scholarly, legal, or professional purposes. Recall takes precedence over precision.

4. Re-finding: The user relies on associative or partial memory to try to locate content they have previously encountered.

Searching is rarely a single action; it is an iterative dialogue between the user and the system. A user may begin with a broad browse, use a term from the results to launch a search, and then apply filters to refine the subset of content. This berrypicking behavior, where information is gathered in bits and pieces from multiple paths, is the norm for complex needs. Designing search in isolation from browsing creates a fractured experience; the two systems must be interwoven to allow seamless transitions.

4.2.4.3 Designing the Search Interface: From Box to Results

The search interface communicates both the user's needs and the site's corpus. Its design must account for the full range of user demands and varying skill levels now recognized.

A one-size-fits-all search box is ineffective for both beginners and specialists. Progressive disclosure provides the solution: for most users, a simple single-query box should be paired with a clear link to an advanced search interface. In this advanced panel, powerful features such as fielded search (title, author, date), Boolean operators, and filters should be readily available, accompanied by examples and intuitive labels. This approach satisfies experts' need for control without overwhelming the average user.

The visual identity and interaction patterns of a website must be seamlessly integrated into the search experience, especially the results pages. A generic results page from an off-the-shelf search engine can feel jarring, disrupting the user's sense of place. For a polished, reliable experience, templates should be customized to align with the site's typography, colors, and components. Equally important as the ranking of results is how they are presented. Effective design must address:

- What to show: Display the most useful identifying metadata (title, relevant snippet, date, type) for each result. A product result should not be presented in the same way as a news item.

- How to arrange: Provide explicit sorting options (date, alphabetical, and relevance) explicit. Be transparent about "relevance" and, where possible, explain the contributing factors (e.g., title matches, freshness).

- How to guide: Always indicate the user's position within the results, the total number of results, and the original query ("Showing 11–20 of 143"). Avoid dead ends for queries that return no results; instead, offer search tips, suggest broader terms, and provide a clear link back to browsing.

4.2.4.4 The Engine Beneath: Smarter Indexing with Search Zones

The most sophisticated interface will fail if the underlying index is poorly constructed. Indexing every word on each page, including navigation footers and sidebar content, clutters the search corpus. The strategic solution is the creation of search zones.

A search zone is a separately indexed portion of site content, defined by a common attribute. Instead of searching a "fruit salad" of mixed material, users can search specifically for "apples" or "oranges," greatly improving relevance. Zones can be organized along several logical dimensions:

- By Content Type: Separate zones for product pages, support articles, blog posts, and press releases. For example, a user seeking troubleshooting assistance should not be overwhelmed with marketing content.
- By Audience: For sites serving multiple groups (e.g., students, faculty, administrators), audience-specific zones ensure that policies for one group do not interfere with results for another.
- By topic or subject: Enable users to search within a defined category that mirrors the site's information structure (for example, "Search within 'Digital Cameras'").
- By Chronology: For news or blog sites, allow users to limit searches to the last 7, 30, or 90 days to respect time-sensitive content.

Implementing zones requires upfront analysis and ongoing content curation, but the payoff is substantial: precise, actionable results that significantly enhance user satisfaction.

4.2.4.5 Search as a Strategic Dialogue

Implementing site search is more than just a technical checkbox; it represents a commitment to fostering a dynamic, supportive dialogue with users. It begins with a strategic decision informed by the scope and type of the content. It necessitates empathy for the diverse and iterative ways in which users seek information. Search must be delivered through a strong yet seamless interface, powered by intelligent indexing method that respects the underlying data structure. When these elements align, search evolves beyond a tool into a foundational component of a useable, valuable, and resilient information ecosystem.

4.3 Principles and Goals of Organizing and Structuring Information

Designers use information architecture to organize content in ways that enhance comprehension, navigation, and task completion. In (Brown, 2010), founder of EightShapes, articulated eight information architecture principles (Figure 4.5). According to Holla, M. (2018), these principles serve as guidelines to help designers make informed decisions about structuring content effectively.

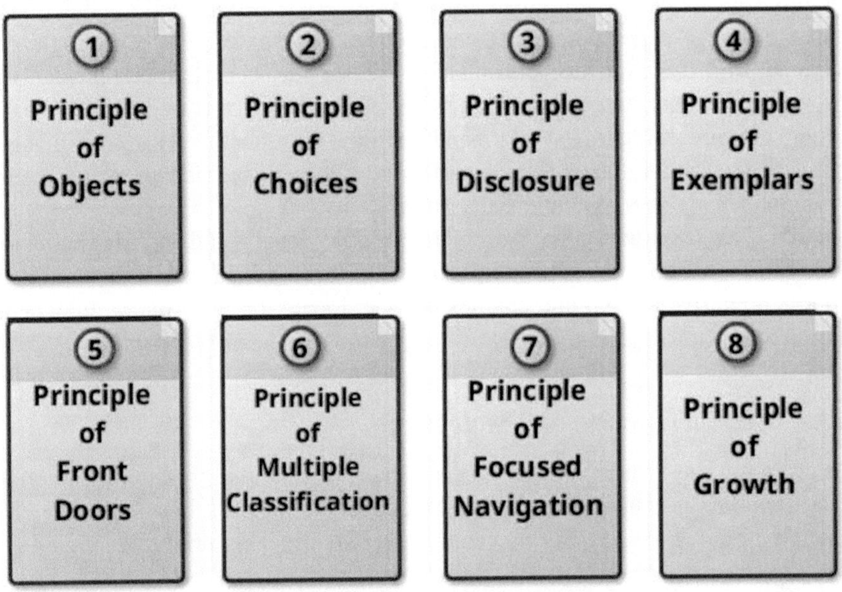

Figure 4.5: Eight principles of information architecture.

4.3.1 *The Principle of Objects*

According to the Principle of Objects, content should be treated as a living entity with a lifecycle, actions, and properties rather than as static text and images. This concept draws inspiration from object-oriented programming, where distinct code segments have methods (behaviors) and properties (attributes). Applied to content, an "object" possesses both a consistent internal structure and a set of behaviors. For example, the predictable structure of a recipe object, ingredients, preparation time, and dietary information, enables advanced sorting and relational features, including linking to related dishes or variations. It can also "reproduce" through user comments that add twists, and its relevance may rise or fall in response to seasonal patterns. By recognizing these object-like characteristics early in a project, information architects can design adaptable, dynamic, and intelligent systems built on relationships and change.

4.3.2 The Principle of Choices

The Principle of Choices emphasizes designing websites that present users with targeted, meaningful options relevant to their current tasks. As explained in the previous chapter that Hick's Law provides the scientific basis, showing that decision time increases with each additional choice. Barry Schwartz's The Paradox of Choice further illustrates that, although people believe they want more alternatives, an excess of options often leads to anxiety, increases cognitive overload, and impaired decision-making. This issue is particularly evident in corporate intranets, where users must sift through unstructured content (e.g., a long, undifferentiated list of benefit policies), frequently resulting in task abandonment and reliance on less effective alternatives such as phone calls. To counter this, the principle calls for a deliberate approach to information hierarchy: distributing content across multiple levels and offering concise targeted lists of options, especially at the top levels of the site structure. This reduces cognitive burden and enables users to locate the information they need more quickly and efficiently.

4.3.3 The Principle of Disclosure

According to the Principle of Disclosure, interfaces should present only enough information to help users understand the deeper content that lies ahead, thereby managing cognitive load and preventing overwhelm. This principle applies the broader concept of progressive disclosure, which recognizes that human attention is finite and that information presented before a user is ready to process it becomes mere noise. In practice, designers must conceptualize information in discrete layers, each offering an appropriate level of detail relevant for its context. For example, a category page on a food website listing seasonal recipes would be ineffective if it displayed the full recipe or unrelated metadata, such as cuisine type. Instead, it provide offer a thoughtful preview, such as the recipe name, an appealing image, and a few key ingredients, giving users just enough background to decide whether to continue. This layered approach fosters intuitive, effective exploration, reduces cognitive effort, and respects the user's attention.

4.3.4 The Principle of Exemplars

The Principle of Exemplars defines categories by illustrating them with examples. This opening captures the essence of the concept: the most effective way to communicate what a category represents is not through an abstract label or a textual definition, but by displaying specific, concrete instances that belong to it. This method provides immediate, tangible context.

Rooted in cognitive science, the principle draws on decades of research into how people categorize information. The rationale is not arbitrary; it reflects scientific insights into human cognition. Studies show that the brain does not store perfect, dictionary-like definitions of categories through networks of remembered examples, particularly the "best" or most typical ones, known as prototypes.

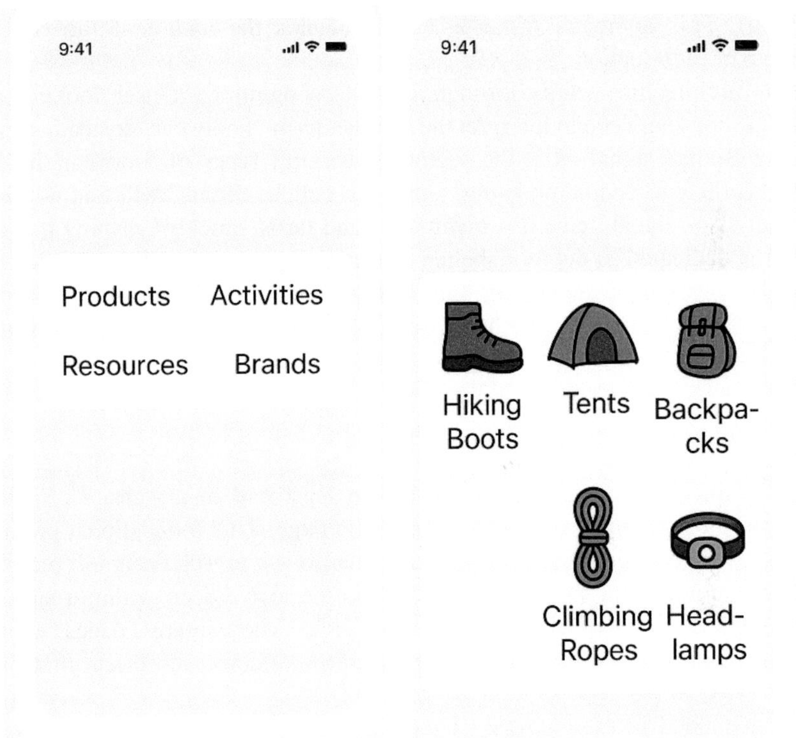

(a) (b)

Figure 4.6: (a) Poor IA violating the principle of exemplars, (b) Good IA using the principle of exemplars.

Poor information architecture that violates the Principle of Exemplars often relies on vague, abstract categories. Main navigation may feature generic labels such as "Products," "Activities," "Resources," or "Brands." This lack of specificity forces users into a cycle of guessing and exploration. For instance, clicking on "Activities" might reveal another layer of ambiguous terms like

"Land-Based," "Water-Based," and "Winter." Such design fails to provide clear mental signposts, requiring users to click repeatedly and construct their own understanding of what content might be hidden within each category. The result is frustration and, often, site abandonment.

In contrast, a good information architecture that applies the Principle of Exemplars employs specific, concrete examples to represent broader categories. Main navigation might feature clear, tangible items like "Hiking Boots" (exemplifying Footwear), "Tents" (exemplifying Shelter), "Backpacks" (exemplifying Packs & Bags), "Climbing Ropes" (exemplifying Climbing Gear), "Camp Stoves" (exemplifying Cooking), and "Headlamps" (exemplifying Lighting). This approach instantly communicates the nature of the content available in each section.

This architecture works through instant recognition: a user looking for "sandals" does not need to interpret the abstract term "Footwear." Instead, seeing "Hiking Boots" signals that the section covers all types of footwear. It also supports efficient mental modeling; a user who clicks "Tents" will find not only tents but also related items like hammocks and tarps, quickly grasping that the section is dedicated to outdoor shelter. Furthermore, it establishes a predictable structure: a user interested in climbing knows to start at "Climbing Ropes" and can confidently expect to find harnesses and there. The result is a system that feels intuitive, consistent, and easy to navigate.

4.3.5 The Principle of Front Doors

The Principle of Front Doors asserts that at least half of a website's visitors will enter through a page other than the home page. This foundational premise challenges the traditional, homepage-centric approach to web design. It reminds designers and content strategists that users often arrive deep within a site via search engines, social media links, or shared URLs. These internal pages become the new "front doors," and must be designed to welcome and orient first-time visitors effectively.

As explained in the previous chapter, Jakob's law that while Jakob's Law and the "Front Doors" Principle are complementary but govern distinct phases of the user experience. Jakob's Law addresses internal interaction patterns: once users are inside a site, they expect navigation, icons, and controls to function consistently with the mental models they have developed from other sites. This ensures intuitive operation and reduces cognitive load. In contrast, the Front Doors Principle (also known as Every Page is Page One, or EPPO) focuses on entry points and information architecture. It recognizes that users often land deep within a site via search engines or shared links, meaning every page must be self-sufficient, providing immediate context, orientation, and clear pathways without assuming the user having seen the homepage. Together, these principles create a seamless journey: the "Front Doors" principle ensures users are not lost upon arrival, while Jakob's Law ensures they can navigate effortlessly once inside.

This principle has become widespread because data from even the largest websites shows that most traffic arrives through "side doors," driven primarily by search engines. It is grounded not in hypothesis but in empirical web analytics. The dominance of search engines like Google as the starting point for most online activity means users often bypass the intended entry point, the home page, and land directly on the page that matches their query. This shift in user behavior requires a corresponding shift in design strategy.

The first practical application of this principle is that every destination page must help users understand where they are and what else the site offers. Every destination page, any page containing the primary content a user seeks (e.g., an article, product, or video), must serve two purposes. First, it must immediately satisfy the user's initial need. Second, it must function as a new home page, providing context about the larger site and clear pathways for further exploration. In essence, it must answer two critical questions: "What is this place?" and "What else can I do here?"

4.3.6 The Principle of Multiple Classification

The Principle of Multiple Classification recommends that designers provide visitors with a variety of classification schemes for browsing a website's content. This principle recognizes that there is no single, "correct" way to organize information that works for every user. Instead, it advocates for creating multiple, complementary pathways, such as by topic, content type, or department, to reflect the diverse ways individuals naturally search for and conceptualize information.

This principle is a practical application of core psychological insights, bridging the gap between rigid information systems and the fluid, varied nature of human cognition. At its core, this approach responds to the fundamental reality that users do not all think alike. Each person arrives at a website with a distinct mental model, an intuitive, pre-existing theory of how the information should be organized. For example, a new employee might view a company intranet as a checklist of "tasks I need to complete," while a long-time manager may see it as a repository of "resources for my team." By offering multiple classification schemes, such as browsing by department, content type, or topic, the design respectfully accommodates these varied internal maps, speaking the user's language rather than forcing them to adopt the system's.

This approach draws deeply on Gestalt principles of perception, which explain how we organize visual elements into coherent wholes. The design enables multiple, equally valid "wholes" to emerge from the same set of information. The Principle of Similarity is applied by allowing users to select their preferred framework for grouping; for instance, "HR Policy" and "Finance

Policy" may be perceived as similar department, while "Policy" and "Form" may be seen as similar by content type. Furthermore, the Figure-Ground Relationship becomes dynamic, as the user determines the focal point, the "figure", whether it is the HR department or the policy document type, while the remaining content recedes into a structured background. This flexibility ultimately supports the Law of Prägnanz (Simplicity), offering a clear and straightforward path that aligns with the user's mental model and reduces cognitive strain.

However, this beneficial flexibility introduces a critical psychological governed by the laws of cognitive load and decision-making. Miller's Law reminds us that human working memory is severely limited, capable of holding only about seven (plus or minus two) items at once. Presenting every possible classification scheme with equal prominence, for example, a navigation bar cluttered with topics, types, departments, audiences, and dates, would quickly overwhelm this capacity. Likewise, Hick's Law demonstrates that decision time increases logarithmically with the number of choices. An overabundance of parallel pathways risks paralyzing users, forcing them to deliberate excessively over which path to take first. The designer's essential role, therefore, is to act as a curator, selecting the two or three most meaningful and useful schemes and implementing them through techniques like progressive disclosure. For instance, a user might first choose "HR" (one decision), which then reveals a sub-menu with "Policies, Forms, News" (a subsequent, smaller decision). This "chunking" of choices effectively manages cognitive load and accelerates decision-making.

4.3.7 The Principle of Focused Navigation

The Principle of Focused Navigation states that a navigation menu should serve a single, clear purpose and avoid mixing different types of links, often described as "apples and oranges." Each navigation mechanism on a page should be dedicated to one specific method of classification or one distinct user goal. Combining unrelated links in a single menu increases cognitive load, confuses users, and makes the site's structure harder to grasp.

The most common mistake this principle prevents is the mixing of unrelated items. Imagine a main menu that lists "Our Products," "About Us," "Client Login," "Contact Sales," and "Job Openings" together. This blend is confusing because it forces users to decipher the menu's hidden logic. Is it meant for learning about the company, or for taking an action? Such ambiguity creates "cognitive load," the mental effort required to understand the system. When users must think too hard about the menu, they become frustrated and may abandon the site.

To apply this principle, designers should separate links into distinct, clearly defined menus. Each menu must be visually differentiated and serve a unique purpose. For example, the main navigation bar at the top of a page should focus on core content, like "Products," "Services," and "Blog." A smaller utility menu at the very top might include "Login," "Search," or "Help." Meanwhile, the footer can house another dedicated menu for less urgent links like "Careers," "Privacy Policy," and "Site Map." This separation creates clarity and provides users with a straightforward path through the site.

Following this principle makes a website immediately more usable and professional. Users can locate information or complete tasks more quickly because they are not forced to sift through a cluttered list. The site's structure becomes easier to learn and remember, while its clarity builds trust, a well-organized site feels more credible and reliable than a chaotic one. Ultimately, by reducing confusion, Focused Navigation keeps users engaged longer and gently guides them toward important actions, such as making a purchase or contacting the organization.

4.3.8 The Principle of Growth

The Principle of Growth asserts that designers must assume the current content represents only a fraction of what will exist in the future. Websites should therefore be designed not merely for their launch state, but for their inevitable evolution. Digital content is never static; it multiplies and diversifies over time, and the architecture must be able to accommodate this expansion gracefully without breaking down or becoming unusable.

This principle is self-evident, content proliferates constantly online, yet it is challenging because designing for unlimited growth is inherently difficult. The root of the issue lies in the nature of the web itself: publishing is easy, storage is inexpensive, so content accumulates relentlessly. The core challenge is tension between the digital and the physical. While server space is virtually limitless, the interface through which information is presented is constrained by human cognition and the physical screen. Users can only process and interact with a limited amount of information at once, making growth a design problem rather than a storage problem.

There are no simple rules for applying this principle because growth is inevitable, but its direction remains unpredictable. A website can expand in three primary, and often simultaneous, ways:

- Volume: Adding more content within existing categories (e.g., additional articles on the same topic).
- Format: Introducing new types of content within existing categories (e.g., incorporating videos into a text-based section).
- Scope: Creating entirely new categories or topics.

The solution is to apply the Principle of Focused Navigation by distributing the responsibility for handling growth across distinct, dedicated parts of the architecture. Rather than relying on a single monolithic system trying to manage every type of expansion, each purpose-built navigation mechanism is designed to address a specific kind of growth:

- A topic-based menu can accommodate the addition of new topics (scope) by using broad top-level categories that can easily house new sub-categories.
- A topic page template can support new content types (format) by being designed from the outset to elegantly display videos, galleries, podcasts, and other media alongside text.

By assigning specific growth responsibilities to different parts of the design, a website can adapt to change gracefully and with minimal disruption. This partitioned strategy makes the system more resilient and easier to maintain. When a new type of content or a new topic needs to be added, designers and developers know exactly which component of the architecture to adjust, without having to redesign the entire site. This approach enables the website to scale "with minimal fuss," ensuring its long-term usability and value.

4.4 Information Architecture Process

In her book A Practical Guide to Information Architecture (Spencer, 2010), Donna Spencer outlines the Information Architecture (IA) process in four primary stages. However, these stages can be expanded into nine for a more comprehensive understanding (Babich N., 2022; uxplanet.org, 2024).

4.4.1 Step 1: Understand the Context & Constraints

Before any organizational decisions can be made, it is essential to develop a comprehensive understanding of the entire ecosystem in which the information architecture will operate. This foundational stage requires a thorough analysis of several key areas. First, business goals must be clarified to ensure the IA directly supports overarching objectives, such as increasing sales, reducing customer support calls, or fostering an online community. Concurrently, practical budget and resource constraints should be assessed, including the project's timeline, financial limitations, and the size and skill set of the team. The technological landscape must be evaluated, including the choice of content management system (CMS) or platform and any technical limitations that may shape the IA's design. Finally, an initial review of the existing content and data is necessary to inventory what information is already available and to assess its accuracy, relevance, and overall quality. The key output of this phase is typically a project charter or

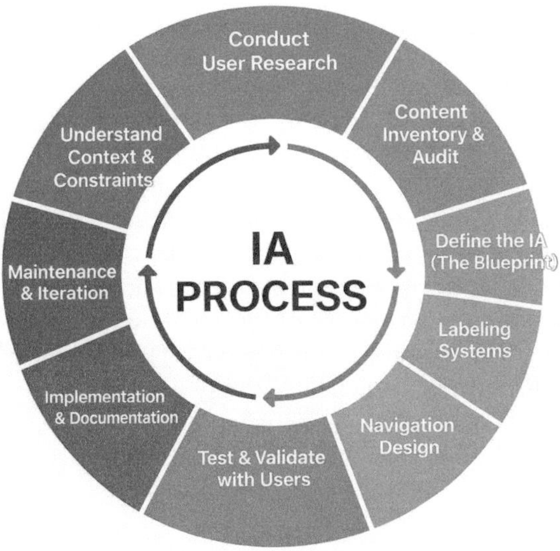

Figure 4.7: Information architecture process.

business requirements document, which serves as a guiding agreement that aligns all stakeholders on the project's purpose, scope, and constraints before moving forward.

4.4.2 Step 2: Conduct User Research

At its core, Information Architecture is about serving users, which makes it essential to deeply understand their needs, behaviors, and mental models. This phase focuses on moving beyond assumptions and gathering direct insights from the people who will interact with the system. A variety of qualitative and quantitative methods, such as user interviews and surveys, provide firsthand accounts of user goals, challenges, and expectations. These insights are often synthesized into personas, fictional representations of key user groups that help keep the design process focused and empathetic. Additionally, user journey maps are created to visualize the steps users take to complete critical tasks, highlighting potential pain points and opportunities for improvement. A cornerstone technique in IA, card sorting, is used to uncover users' natural mental models of information. In an open card sort, participants group content and create their own category labels, which is ideal for new projects. In a closed card sort, users sort content into pre-defined categories, making it effective for validating an existing structure. The key outputs of this research phase, personas, journey maps, and card sort results, provide a robust, evidence-based foundation for making informed structural decisions in subsequent design stages.

4.4.3 Step 3: Content Inventory & Audit

After understanding user needs, the next critical step is to take a comprehensive inventory of all existing content through a systematic content audit. This process begins with a quantitative inventory, which entails creating a complete, spreadsheet-based list of every page, document, and digital asset within the current ecosystem, answering the fundamental question, "What do we have?" Once the full scope is mapped, a qualitative audit is conducted. This stage critically evaluates each content item against criteria such as accuracy, relevance to user and business goals, consistency of tone, and overall usefulness, thereby addressing the essential question, "Is it any good?" The key output of this phase is a detailed spreadsheet or report that not only catalogs all content but also provides actionable recommendations on what to keep, revise, consolidate, or discard. This evidence base is crucial for shaping structure and guiding the content migration strategy.

4.4.4 Step 4: Define the IA (The Blueprint)

Building on the insights gained from user research and content analysis, this phase represents the core design effort where the conceptual structure of the information environment is created. It involves defining several interrelated components that together form the architectural blueprint. First, organization schemes are established to determine how information will be categorized, by topic, task, audience, or chronology, ensuring that content is grouped in intuitive ways. Simultaneously, overarching organization structures are selected, typically combining a primary hierarchical/tree model for main navigation, with sequential structures for linear processes and matrix structures that allow users to access content through multiple filters. These decisions are crystallized in a sitemap, which provides a visual diagram of the website's page hierarchy and relationships. To support detailed findability, a taxonomy and metadata schema is developed, creating a controlled vocabulary for tagging content and defining attributes that enable advanced search and filtering. Finally, these structural choices are translated into wireframes, low-fidelity layouts that specify how navigation systems and content blocks will be arranged on individual pages. The key outputs of this comprehensive phase, the sitemap, taxonomy, and wireframes, serve as the essential blueprint guiding all subsequent design and development work.

4.4.5 Step 5: Labeling Systems

With the structural blueprint in place, the focus shifts to developing clear and consistent labeling systems that enable users to navigate and understand the information architecture effectively. This critical phase involves creating intuitive labels for navigation menus, categories, and headings that reflect the user's language rather than relying on internal jargon or technical terminology. The goal is to ensure labels are immediately understandable and accurately represent the content they describe, allowing users to predict what they will find before clicking. For example, ambiguous terms like "Asset Management" might be replaced with the more descriptive "Photo Gallery," while the user-centered label "Services" is preferable to the vague corporate term "Solutions." This process typically includes reviewing the taxonomy and sitemap, testing label options with users, and establishing a consistent style guide for terminology. The key output is a defined set of approved navigation and heading labels that create a coherent language system throughout the digital product, significantly enhancing findability and user comprehension.

4.4.6 Step 6: Navigation Design

Following the establishment of the structural blueprint and labeling system, the next critical phase involves designing comprehensive navigation systems that allow users to move seamlessly through the information architecture. This process focuses on creating multiple, interconnected wayfinding mechanisms that accommodate different user behaviors and needs. The foundation is typically the global navigation, the primary menu system visible across all pages, providing consistent access to main content areas. This is complemented by local navigation, which offers contextual menus specific to a section, such as a sidebar with sub-pages or related links. Additionally, utility navigation provides access to key functional actions like Login, Contact, and Search, usually positioned in secondary locations such as the top header. To enhance user orientation within the hierarchical structure, breadcrumbs are implemented as a visual trail that shows the user's current location relative to the site's organization. Finally, search functionality is carefully designed, encompassing both the placement and behavior of the search box as well as the layout and relevance of the search results page. The key output of this phase is a set of detailed navigation specifications, integrated into and visualized through wireframes, ensuring a cohesive and intuitive user experience.

4.4.7 Step 7: Test & Validate with Users

Before committing resources to development, it is essential to test and validate the proposed information architecture with real users to ensure it functions as intended. This critical phase employs rigorous evaluation methods to identify potential usability issues while they can still be easily corrected. A primary technique is tree testing, in which participants are presented with a text-only version of the site structure and asked to locate specific items or complete tasks. This method isolates the findability of information, providing clear data on the effectiveness of the categorization and labeling without the influence of visual design. Additionally, usability testing is conducted using interactive wireframes or prototypes to assess whether users can complete key tasks within the more realistic context of a simulated interface. The key output of this phase is a comprehensive test report that documents findings, highlights areas of confusion or failure, and provides actionable recommendations for refining the architecture, navigation, and labeling before moving to the implementation stage.

4.4.8 Step 8: Implementation & Documentation

Once the information architecture has been validated through user testing, the focus shifts to implementation and comprehensive documentation to ensure the design is accurately realized. This phase requires close collaboration between developers and content creators to translate the architectural blueprint into a functional product. Key activities include preparing detailed IA documentation that provides the development team with all necessary specifications, such as the final sitemap, annotated wireframes, taxonomy schemas, and content models. For redesign projects, a critical component is content migration planning, which outlines the process for moving, adapting, and integrating existing content into the new structure while preserving integrity and metadata. The key output of this phase is a complete package of finalized IA deliverables that serves as the single source of truth for all stakeholders involved in the build process, ensuring alignment and fidelity to the designed user experience throughout development.

4.4.9 Step 9: Maintenance & Iteration

The launch of a website or application marks the beginning of an ongoing process of maintenance and iteration, as a robust information architecture is a living system that must evolve alongside user needs and business objectives. This final, continuous phase involves actively monitoring the system's performance through analytics to understand how users actually behave, identifying where they encounter obstacles, what content they search for most frequently, and which paths they take to complete tasks. These quantitative insights are complemented by qualitative feedback loops established through user surveys, support channel monitoring, and direct user testing, which provide context for the behaviors observed in the data. A proactive content strategy ensures that content is continuously evaluated, added, updated, or archived in accordance with established IA and governance rules, preventing structural decay. The key output is not a static document but a cycle of ongoing, evidence-based updates and refinements to the architecture, ensuring it remains effective, relevant, and scalable over time.

4.5 Conclusion

Information Architecture (IA) is the strategic backbone of effective UX design, transforming raw content into coherent, navigable, and meaningful user experiences through the intentional structuring of organizational, labeling, navigation, and search systems. Grounded in cognitive psychology and user-centered design principles, IA bridges the gap between user mental models and business objectives, enabling intuitive access to information while reducing cognitive load. To build scalable and resilient information environments, the discipline employs a systematic, iterative approach that includes contextual analysis and user research, blueprint creation, testing, and ongoing maintenance. When executed effectively, IA operates seamlessly in the background, fostering user trust and satisfaction by ensuring that digital environments are not only useable but also adaptive, supporting both immediate tasks and sustained engagement within evolving digital ecosystems.

Chapter 5

Interaction Design

The next step is to define how users will interact with the structure once it has been established and is psychologically sound. How does a menu open? What kind of feedback can a button provide? Interaction design focuses on the specific actions and exchanges that occur between the user and the product. At its core, interaction design is about shaping the way people engage with digital products. Its goal is to develop software such as websites or applications, that enables users to accomplish their goals effectively. This broad discipline encompasses motion, sound, space, aesthetics, and other factors, each requiring specialized knowledge. While UX design also incorporates user research, persona creation, and usability testing to shape the overall experience, it shares many similarities with interaction design, which emphasizes the mechanics of user-product interaction.

5.1 The Five Dimensions of Interaction Design: An Integrated Framework

The Five Dimensions framework offers a comprehensive approach to interaction design, with each dimension addressing distinct aspects of the user experience while working in concert with the others. This integrated approach ensures that designs account for everything from microinteractions to environmental context. Table 5.1 illustrates how the dimensions collaborate to create seamless experiences.

This methodology requires designers to evaluate all dimensions concurrently rather than sequentially. For example, designing a form submission (Words) involves clear labels and error messages, complemented by visual feedback

DOI: 10.1201/9781003715764-5

Table 5.1: The five dimensions of interaction design: Interrelationships and applications.

Dimension	Primary Focus	Key Questions	Related Design Principles
Words	Semantic meaning and clarity	What language does the user understand? How can text guide actions?	Clarity, consistency, plain language, action-oriented verb
Visual Representations	Perception and aesthetics	How do visual elements guide attention? What establishes hierarchy and relationships?	Visual hierarchy, contrast, alignment, gestalt principles
Physical Objects/Space	Tangibility and context	What device is being used? Where and how is the product being used?	Ergonomics, contextual design, adaptive interfaces
Time	Change and progress	How long do actions take? How is feedback timed? What indicates progress?	Feedback loops, timing, pacing, progressive disclosure
Behavior	Functionality and intelligence	How does the system respond? What makes interactions feel intelligent?	Affordances, signifiers, mappings, system intelligence

(Visual Representations), consideration of whether the form is being completed on a mobile device in motion (Physical Objects/Space), appropriate validation timing (Time), and intelligent autofill or error prevention (Behavior). The most effective interaction designs emerge when all five dimensions are aligned with user needs and contextual demands.

5.2 The First Dimension - Words

The Dimension of Language and Meaning

Words act as the fundamental link between user intent and system response in digital products. Every label, instruction, error message, and button language provides an opportunity either to clarify or to confuse. In an age when users frequently abandon interfaces due to frustration or misunderstanding, strategic language use has a direct impact on usability, trust, and task completion [citation:2]. This dimension translates abstract functionality into clear, simple communication that users can confidently navigate.

5.2.1 Clarity & Simplicity

Speak the User's Language, not the System's

The primary principle of using proper words in user interface design is to consistently speak the user's language, rather than the system's. This requires translating technical jargon and internal terminology into simple, understandable language that aligns with the user's perspective and objectives. For example, a system-centric error message such as "Incorrect credentials," is vague and ineffective. A more user-centric alternative, "The email or password you entered is incorrect", uses the exact labels visible on the screen, clearly identifies the issue, and implicitly directs the user toward a solution, such as double-checking their entries or clicking the "Forgot password?" link. Similarly, the common phrase "Full Name" should replace jargon like "Nomenclature," following the principle of substituting familiar terms for obscure ones. In the same way, a system-oriented directive such as "Initiate sync protocol" should be translated into the user-friendly command "Sync now." By adopting this approach, the interface not only clarifies the cause of the issues but also guides users intuitively toward solutions, such as password recovery or re-entry attempts, thereby reducing frustration and improving usability.

5.2.2 Conciseness

Every Unnecessary Word Creates Friction

Conciseness is a key discipline in user interface design, aimed at respecting the user's time and reducing cognitive load. In an age of information overload, every unnecessary word introduces friction. The goal is to be highly efficient, eliminating superfluous language, passive voice, and repetition, so that only the essential idea remains. For example, a lengthy warning such as "It appears that you are attempting to perform an action..." is far less direct than the concise alternative, "Permanently delete this file?", a reduction of 87% in text. Similarly, the status message "We have received your request and it is currently being processed..." can be streamlined to "Request received." Processing... for a 60% decrease. Another example: "Please ensure that all required fields have been filled out..." becomes the more actionable "Complete all required fields to continue.", cutting the length by 50%. Short versions can be scanned in seconds, with meaning and importance immediately clear, allowing users to act without wading through a wall of words. Concision improves scanning, speeds comprehension, and enables more confident decision-making. This principle is especially critical in contexts such as error messages, warnings, and instructions, where indecision can lead to mistakes or abandonment.

5.2.3 Action-Oriented Language

Make Outcomes Predictable through Specific Verbs

Action-Oriented Language is essential for making interactive aspects predictable and trustworthy. Buttons and links act as calls to action, and their labels must make the intended outcome clear. An ambiguous label such as "Process" on a form leaves users uncertain, does it submit the form, calculate a total, or generate a report. This ambiguity leads to hesitation. In contrast, explicit, verb-first labels eliminate confusion. For instance, a primary button should read "Save Changes" instead of "Process," a form submission should say "Create Account" instead of "Submit," a file operation should use "Download Report" instead of "Go," and a secondary action should be labeled "View Details" rather than "More." Effective action-oriented labels follow clear patterns: they begin with a verb, such as "Download," "Save," "Create," or "Share"; they are specific, e.g., "Save Draft" when multiple save options exist; they align with user goals, e.g., "Pay Invoice" instead of "Process Payment"; they establish hierarchy, with stronger verbs for primary actions and lighter ones for secondary actions. By setting clear expectations, these labels instill confidence and enable faster, more decisive user actions.

5.2.4 Appropriate Tone & Voice

Humanize Digital Interactions through Emotional Intelligence

Appropriate tone and voice personalize the digital experience and connect with users on an emotional level. Although often used interchangeably, voice and tone are not the same. Voice represents a brand's consistent personality, it may be authoritative, helpful, professional, or playful. Tone, by contrast, is the nuanced adaptation of that voice to a specific context. To illustrate the distinction: voice is defined by a constant personality across all interactions, while tone reflects an emotional response to unique situations. Their durations differ as well, voice is long-term and steady, whereas tone is transient and contextual. For example, a system's voice might be "friendly and encouraging," but its tone would shift depending on the circumstance: empathic in an error message ("We couldn't find that page. Let's bring you back on track."), congratulatory after an accomplishment ("Your masterpiece is finished!"), or urgent in a warning. Aligning tone with context demonstrates empathy and reinforces the user's emotional state, transforming a transactional interaction into something relatable and human-centered.

5.2.5 Consistency

Build Reliable Mental Models through Predictable Language

Consistency is the glue that binds all these concepts together, creating a cohesive and learnable system. It requires that the same phrase be used for the same concept or action throughout the application. Inconsistency, such as using "Remove," "Delete," and "Archive" interchangeably for the same operation, introduces uncertainty and erodes user trust, as users can no longer predict the outcome. A consistent strategy establishes a reliable mental model. For instance, "Delete" should always indicate permanent removal, while "Archive" should consistently mean temporary concealment.

To resolve common inconsistencies, solutions must be applied systematically. For removal actions, ambiguous labels such as "Delete," "Remove," and "Trash" should be standardized: use "Delete" for permanent removal and "Archive" for temporary concealment. This eliminates uncertainty about outcomes. Similarly, inconsistent navigation terms like "Profile," "My Account," and "Settings" should be unified under "Account Settings," ensuring clarity about where users can manage their preferences. For content categories, titles such as "Articles," "Posts," and "Content" should be standardized to "Posts" when referring to user-generated material, making related items easier to identify.

Maintaining this standard requires creating a content dictionary to document approved terms for common actions and concepts, establishing synonym rings to group related terms under a single preferred label, incorporating pattern libraries that include verbal patterns alongside visual UI patterns, and conducting regular consistency audits to detect terminology drift. The power of consistency lies in its cumulative effect: each instance of predictable language reinforces user confidence, gradually building a system that feels reliable and trustworthy over time.

5.2.6 Applied Techniques for Effective UX Writing

Beyond understanding principles, effective implementation requires specific techniques tailored to different interface contexts. Table 5.2 provides actionable strategies for applying the five language principles across common interface elements.

Table 5.2: Applied UX writing techniques for common interface contexts.

Interface Context	Effective Techniques	Common Pitfalls to Avoid
Navigation & Menus	- Use familiar, predictable labels ("Sales Reports" not "Data Insights") - Front-load important words in menu items - Maintain consistent information architecture	- Vague or clever labels requiring interpretation - Inconsistent grouping or categorization - Mixing user actions with content categories
Forms & Inputs	- Clear field labels using everyday language - Inline validation with specific guidance - Examples in placeholders (with persistent labels) - Progressive disclosure for complex forms	- Placeholder text as only label (disappears on input) - Vague error messages ("Invalid input") - Technical jargon in instructions - Asking for unnecessary information
Empty States	- Explain why the space is empty - Provide clear next-step actions - Use encouraging, helpful tone - Include imagery that supports the message	- Bare "No data" messages without guidance - Dead ends with no actionable next steps - Overly technical explanations of emptiness - Missed onboarding opportunities
Error Messages	- Plain language explaining what happened - Specific cause identification - Constructive recovery suggestions - Appropriate tone (not blaming the user)	- Technical error codes without translation - Vague statements ("Something went wrong") - Blaming language ("You entered the wrong...") - No recovery path or next steps
Success Messages	- Clear confirmation of what was accomplished - Relevant next-step suggestions - Appropriate celebratory tone - Option to undo if applicable	- Generic confirmations ("Success!") - Missing closure or next-step guidance - Overly enthusiastic tone for minor actions - No way to review or edit completed action

5.2.7 Implementing the Words Dimension: A Structured Approach

Applying these principles systematically requires moving beyond ad-hoc decisions to establishing clear guidelines and processes:

1. **Content Audit & Analysis:** Review existing interface text to identify inconsistencies, jargon, and unclear messaging. Analyze user feedback, support tickets, and usability test findings related to language issues.

2. **User Language Research:** Conduct research to understand how users naturally describe tasks, concepts, and problems. Methods may include

user interviews, diary studies, customer support transcript analysis, and card sorting exercises.

3. **Style Guide Development:** Create a comprehensive content style guide that covers voice and tone guidelines, terminology standards, grammar and punctuation rules, and format specifications for different interface elements.
4. **Implementation & Pattern Library:** Develop reusable text patterns for common interface elements (error messages, empty states, success messages, etc.) and integrate them into the design system to ensure consistent application across products.
5. **Testing & Iteration:** Validate language choices with real users through methods such as cloze tests (fill-in-the-blank), comprehension tests, and A/B testing of different phrasing. Monitor analytics to identify friction points related to language.

The cumulative effect of consistent, clear, and thoughtful language across an interface builds user confidence and trust. Each instance of predictable wording strengthens the user's mental model of how the system works, reducing anxiety and improving efficiency. In this way, the Words dimension functions both as the foundation of usability and as the primary medium through which brand personality and values are conveyed.

5.3 The Second Dimension – Visual Representations

The Dimension of Perception and Aesthetics

This aspect goes beyond simple utility, transforming a logical arrangement of words into an engaging and intuitive experience. The product's look, feel, and silent guidance form its visual language, which leverages our natural ability to process visual information. By applying fundamental principles of perception, psychology, and hierarchy, visual language builds trust, directs attention, and makes the interface not only functional but also compelling. Let's examine the most important factors.

5.3.1 Typography

Typography in user interface design is far more than the superficial choice of an attractive font. It serves as a fundamental structural tool that establishes both visual hierarchy and brand tone. By strategically employing type, designers create an invisible guide that directs the user's attention and shapes perceptions of the product's character before a single word is consciously read.

One of typography's primary purposes is to establish a clear visual hierarchy, achieved by varying font size, weight, and style. Similar to the semantic framework offered by HTML tags ($< h1 >$, $< h2 >$, $< p >$), this approach generates a scannable information architecture that helps users quickly understand relationships between content and identify what is most important. For example, subheadings may use a smaller, semi-bold treatment; prominent headlines draw attention with large, bold type; and body text provides the foundation with regular weight and optimal spacing. This logical progression acts as the eye's invisible guide. Table 5.3 demonstrates how a consistent typographic scale translates abstract content structures into a concrete visual formats. By reducing cognitive strain, this hierarchy facilitates effective scanning and navigation while strengthening the interface's overall logic.

Table 5.3: Typographic hierarchy for user interfaces.

Element	Typical Treatment	Purpose
H1/Headline	32px, Bold, Primary Color	Establish primary focus and page purpose
H2/Subheading	24px, Semi-Bold	Group related content sections
H3/Section Title	18px, Medium	Break down complex information
Body Text	16px, Regular, 1.5 Line Height	Ensure comfortable reading experience
Caption/Label	14px, Light or Medium	Provide supporting information

The practical issue of readability is more important than hierarchy. This entails choosing typefaces that are readable across long sections, with serif or sans-serif fonts picked especially for how well they work on screens. Additionally, crucial modifications to line height (leading) and letter spacing (tracking) guarantee that the text is neither crowded nor too scattered, resulting in a comfortable reading experience that keeps users interested and reduces eye strain. According to Table 5.4, readability is a measurable discipline. Adhering to its guidelines reduces cognitive strain, enabling users to focus on the material itself rather than struggling with its presentation. Readability serves as the fundamental foundation that supports higher-level functions such as hierarchy and brand expression.

Table 5.4: Readability best practices for digital interfaces.

Factor	Best Practice	Impact on Users
Font Choice	Sans-serif for UI (e.g., Inter, Roboto)	Better screen legibility at various sizes
Line Length	45–75 characters per line	Optimal reading rhythm and eye movement
Line Height	1.4–1.6 × font size	Prevents text crowding, improves scanning
Contrast	Minimum 4.5:1 for body text	Ensures accessibility for all users
Font Weight	Regular (400) for body, Bold (700) for emphasis	Creates clear text differentiation

Typography is the quiet conductor of user experience. It begins by establishing a distinct visual hierarchy to guide attention and clarify the information structure. Building on this foundation, it applies the exacting science of readability to ensure content is easily understood. Through the expressive use of form and spacing, typography conveys brand identity and gives the interface its unique voice. When used purposefully, it transcends mere aesthetics to become an invisible yet essential framework, one that fosters trust, reduces cognitive load, and transforms functional interaction into a cohesive, memorable dialogue between the user and the product.

5.3.2 Icons: The Visual Shorthand of UI

Icons are an interface's essential visual shorthand, designed to provide a nearly universal language that users can quickly understand. Their primary function is to use simple, graphical symbols to represent actions, objects, or concepts across linguistic and cultural boundaries. A single, well-designed icon can replace a word or phrase, conserving screen space and accelerating navigation, making visual communication more effective and user-friendly.

The most important rule in icon design is to prioritize clarity over originality. The ultimate goal is quick and accurate recognition. While creative flair has its place, it must never compromise the icon's core purpose. For example, the "hamburger menu" icon (≡) has become a standardized symbol for hidden navigation menus; replacing it with an abstract or unfamiliar design would likely confuse users and reduce usability. Table 5.5 illustrates some of the standard icons commonly used in interface design.

Table 5.5: Standard icons and user expectations.

Function	Standard Icon	User Expectation
Menu/Navigation	≡ (Hamburger)	Hidden navigation drawer
Search		Search functionality
Settings		Configuration options
Delete/Remove		Permanent deletion
Edit		Modify existing content
Share		Distribute content to others

Visual consistency across an entire icon set is essential for maintaining a cohesive and polished user experience. Every icon within a product should follow the same design language, including a unified color scheme, consistent line weight, a shared approach to corner styling (rounded or sharp), and a standardized method of being filled, outlined, or two-toned. This consistency not only strengthens brand identity but also prevents users from being distracted by sporadic style shifts when moving between screens. Ultimately, it creates a predictable visual environment that feels reliable and seamless.

5.3.3 Images & Illustrations

Images and illustrations in user interface design serve two primary, distinct purposes: functional communication and emotional connection. Functional visuals deliver information directly and aid comprehension, while emotional visuals shape user perception and foster a deeper relationship with the brand. Knowing when to apply each type is essential for using visuals strategically rather than merely decoratively.

Functional visuals are primarily utilitarian, with the goal of explaining, informing, or providing essential context. For example, a screenshot in a help article directly shows users exactly where to click, a diagram simplifies a complex workflow or data set, and a high-quality product photo on an e-commerce site acts as a digital substitute for physical inspection. These images are critical to user success because they reduce ambiguity, answer specific questions, and support practical goals.

In contrast, emotional visuals are employed to evoke feelings, build atmosphere, and establish a brand's personality. A hero image on a homepage featuring happy, diverse people using a service fosters a sense of community and aspiration. Custom illustrations can give a brand a unique, friendly, and approachable character that stock photography cannot replicate. Similarly, a background video of a serene landscape or an adventurous journey instantly sets a mood that resonates with users on a subconscious level.

The most effective interfaces often integrate both functional and emotional visuals to create a holistic experience. For instance, a financial app may present clean, clear data visualizations (functional) on its main dashboard, while employing warm, trustworthy illustrations during onboarding (emotional) to ease user anxiety. This combination ensures the interface is not only usable and clear but also engaging and memorable, ultimately fostering stronger user loyalty.

5.3.4 Color

Color is one of the most powerful tools in a designer's arsenal, carrying the dual responsibility of conveying functional information and evoking psychological responses. On a practical level, it guides user behavior and communicates system status; on a subconscious level, it shapes the user's emotional perception of the brand and product. This dual nature makes strategic color choices essential for creating interfaces that are not only usable but also resonant and trustworthy.

From a functional standpoint, color serves as a highly efficient communication system within the interface. It provides immediate, non-verbal cues about state and interactivity. Universal conventions, such as red for errors or destructive actions, yellow for warnings, and green for success, allow users to assess situations instantly, as shown in Table 5.6. Color is also fundamental in signaling interactivity. Distinct hues for primary buttons and hyperlinks differentiate them from static text and background elements, ensuring users can quickly identify what is clickable.

Table 5.6: Standard color conventions for user interfaces.

Status	**Standard Color**	**Additional Indicators**
Error/Destructive	Red (#DC3545)	Warning icon, clear label
Warning/Caution	Yellow (#FFC107)	Alert icon, explanatory text
Success/Positive	Green (#28A745)	Checkmark icon, confirmation message
Information/Neutral	Blue (#007BFF)	Info icon, descriptive text
Disabled/Inactive	Gray (#6C757D)	Reduced opacity, changed cursor

Beyond its functional role, color is central to branding and emotional impact (Lischer, B. (2024)). A brand's color palette becomes a core part of its identity, making it instantly recognizable, such as Facebook's blue, Spotify's green, or Coca-Cola's red. Psychologically, different hues evoke distinct emotions: blue can instill calm and trust, yellow conveys energy and optimism, and black suggests luxury and sophistication. This emotional dimension helps create atmosphere and fosters a deeper connection with the user, as illustrated in Table 5.7.

Table 5.7: Color psychology in branding: Emotional associations and applications.

Color	Positive Associations	Negative Associations	Brand Examples	Recommended Industries
Red	Power Passion Energy Excitement Fearlessness	Anger Danger Warning Aggression Pain	Coca-Cola, Netflix, Target, YouTube, CNN	Fast Food, Entertainment, Retail Sales, Media, Emergency Services
Orange	Courage Confidence Warmth Innovation Friendliness Energy	Deprivation Frustration Frivolity Immaturity Ignorance	Nickelodeon, Fanta, Harley-Davidson, Amazon, SoundCloud	Youth Brands, Creative Industries, Call-to-Action Buttons, Value Retail, Transportation
Yellow	Optimism Warmth Happiness Creativity Intellect Extraversion	Irrationality Fear Caution Anxiety Frustration Cowardice	McDonald's, IKEA, National Geographic, Post-it, Hertz	Attention-Grabbing Designs, Children's Products, Creativity-Focused Brands, Transportation, Education
Green	Health Hope Freshness Nature Growth Prosperity	Boredom Stagnation Envy Blandness Enervation Sickness	Starbucks, Whole Foods, Spotify, John Deere, Land Rover	Eco-Friendly Brands, Health/Wellness, Finance, Agriculture, Outdoor Recreation
Turquoise	Communication Clarity Calmness Inspiration Self-expression Healing	Boastfulness Secrecy Unreliability Reticence Fence-sitting Aloofness	Tiffany & Co., GoDaddy, Siemens, Roblox, Hisense	Technology, Communication Services, Healthcare, Creative Agencies, Cleaning Products

Continued on next page

Table 5.7: Color psychology in branding: Emotional associations and applications (Continued).

Color	Positive Associations	Negative Associations	Brand Examples	Recommended Industries
Blue	Trust Loyalty Dependability Logic Serenity Security	Coldness Aloofness Emotionless Unfriendliness Uncaring Unappetizing	Facebook, IBM, Samsung, PayPal, Ford, Intel	Finance, Technology, Healthcare, Corporate, Social Media, Automotive
Purple	Wisdom Luxury Wealth Spirituality Imagination Sophistication	Introversion Decadence Suppression Inferiority Extravagance Moodiness	Cadbury, Yahoo!, Hallmark, Roku, FedEx, Twitch	Luxury Goods, Beauty, Spiritual/Wellness, Creative Arts, Confectionery
Magenta	Imagination Passion Transformation Creativity Innovation Balance	Outrageousness Nonconformity Flippancy Impulsiveness Eccentricity Ephemeralness	T-Mobile, Cosmopolitan, LG, Barbie, Indiegogo, PINK	Youthful Brands, Fashion, Media, Disruptive Tech, Beauty Products
Brown	Seriousness Warmth Earthiness Reliability Support Authenticity	Humorlessness Heaviness Lack of sophistication Sadness Dirtiness Conservativeness	UPS, Hershey's, M&M's, Louis Vuitton, Crayola, Godiva	Logistics, Natural/Organic Products, Rugged Apparel, Chocolate, Craftsmanship
Black	Sophistication Security Power Elegance Authority Substance	Oppression Coldness Menace Heaviness Evil Mourning	Chanel, Nike, Apple, Sony, Mercedes-Benz, The New York Times	Luxury Fashion, High-End Tech, Premium Automotive, Publishing, Minimalist Design

Continued on next page

Table 5.7: Color psychology in branding: Emotional associations and applications (Continued).

Color	Positive Associations	Negative Associations	Brand Examples	Recommended Industries
Gray	Timelessness Neutrality Reliability Balance Intelligence Strength	Lack of confidence Dampness Depression Hibernation Lack of energy Blandness	Apple, Mercedes-Benz, Wikipedia, Nintendo, Swarovski, Shopify	Technology, Industrial Design, Luxury (as secondary color), Professional Services, E-commerce
White	Cleanness Clarity Purity Simplicity Sophistication Freshness	Sterility Coldness Unfriendliness Elitism Isolation Emptiness	Apple, Adidas, Tesla, World Health Organization, Converse, Chanel	Healthcare, Technology, Minimalist Brands, Wedding/Bridal Industry, Sportswear

Perhaps the most critical consideration in color application is accessibility. Color should never be the sole means of conveying information, as this excludes users with color vision deficiencies. For instance, an error message should not only appear in red but also include an icon or text label. Equally important is maintaining sufficient contrast between text and its background. Strong contrast is non-negotiable for readability, ensuring that all users, including those with low vision, can comfortably consume content. By adhering to these principles, designers create interfaces that are inclusive, usable, and accessible to the entire audience.

5.3.5 Layout & Spacing

Layout and spacing form the structural foundation of any user interface, creating order and significantly reducing cognitive load. By thoughtfully arranging elements and managing the space between them, designers can transform a chaotic collection of components into a clear, navigable, and intuitive environment. This structural integrity makes an interface feel stable, intentional, and easy to interpret at a glance.

5.3.5.1 *Grid System*

Grid systems provide the essential structural framework for organizing elements on a page. By establishing visual consistency and alignment, grids transform chaotic content into clear, navigable interfaces that are both aesthetically pleasing and functionally effective. According to Gordon, K. (2022), three core grid structures underpin digital interfaces.

1. Column Grid

UI elements are aligned to the vertical columns that structure a page. Across layouts, this simple yet effective system establishes rhythm and order. It is particularly well-suited for blogs, articles, content-heavy websites, and organized applications. Its defining feature is the creation of consistent vertical alignment and uniform spacing.

2. Modular Grid

The column grid can be extended by adding horizontal rows, creating modules at the points where they intersect. These consistent containers organize content into predictable, repeating patterns. This structure is particularly effective for e-commerce platforms, galleries, dashboards, and listing pages, as it provides uniform containers that support browsing, comparison, and clarity.

3. Hierarchical Grid

Content is organized by importance, with the most significant elements occupying larger grid areas. This structure promotes natural visual flow and directs focus effectively. It is particularly well-suited for news sites, editorial layouts, and interfaces that rely on a strong visual hierarchy. Key characteristics include prioritizing material based on relevance and user engagement.

5.3.5.2 *Space System*

White space, or negative space, refers to the empty areas between and around elements, often misunderstood as wasted space. In reality, it is a critical design element in its own right. When used strategically, white space reduces visual clutter, groups related items through the principle of proximity, and separates unrelated ones. Most importantly, it gives content room to breathe, dramatically improving readability, focus, and the overall aesthetic appeal of the interface.

A successful layout establishes a clear visual flow, strategically guiding the user's eye through content in a logical and intentional sequence. For example, on a landing page, the design may lead the eye from the logo in the top-left corner, to a compelling headline, then to a supporting image, and finally to the primary call-to-action button. This controlled journey ensures that users encounter the

Table 5.8: Standard spacing scale for UI design.

Spacing Unit	Use Case	Visual Effect
4px/8px	Internal padding, icon spacing	Tight grouping, compact feel
16px/24px	Between related elements	Clear grouping, comfortable separation
32px/48px	Between major sections	Strong visual separation, breathing room
64px/96px	Page/screen margins	Dramatic focus, premium feel

most important information in the right order, facilitating comprehension and driving engagement.

The golden rule that unites all visual elements, layout, typography, color, and icons, into a cohesive whole is consistency. This principle ensures the interface behaves and appears as a unified system rather than a collection of disjointed parts. To maintain this cohesion, teams often develop a design system or style guide, serving as a single source of truth for the product's visual and interactive language.

5.4 The Third Dimension – Physical Objects/Space

The Dimension of Tangibility and Context

The Third Dimension acknowledges a fundamental truth often overlooked in digital design: all human, computer interactions occur within physical reality. While the First Dimension (Words) establishes semantic meaning and the Second Dimension (Visual Representations) creates perceptual understanding, this third dimension grounds digital experiences in the tangible world of devices, environments, and human physiology.

Digital interfaces do not exist in isolation, they are experienced through physical hardware, in specific locations, under particular environmental conditions, and within the limitations and capabilities of the human body. For instance, a user accessing a banking app on a crowded subway during their morning commute faces fundamentally different constraints than someone using the same app on a desktop computer in a quiet home office. This dimension requires designers to move beyond pixel-perfect screen designs and consider how digital experiences translate into physical reality.

Every interaction represents a dialogue between human physical capabilities, technological hardware constraints, and environmental conditions. Designing with this triad in mind captures the essence of the Third Dimension.

5.4.1 The Physical Object: Medium of Interaction

Every digital interface is accessed through a physical object whether a smartphone held in the hand, a mouse resting on a desk, or a VR controller used in three-dimensional space. This tangible intermediary is not merely a passive conduit but an active participant in the interaction, imposing distinct ergonomic, functional, and cognitive constraints upon the user. The design of a digital experience, therefore, cannot be considered complete or effective without a thorough understanding of the physical medium through which it will be engaged. The properties of the device fundamentally shape the interaction method, dictating everything from the optimal size of interactive targets to the types of gestures that feel natural and intuitive.

Physical devices impose both technological and anatomical limits. For example, the average contact area of a human fingertip is about 10 millimeters, which corresponds to a minimum touch target size of 44 x 44 pixels on a screen with standard density. Tiny, closely spaced interface elements on touchscreens are frustrating and error-prone because of this biological constraint. Conversely, smaller targets and complex interactions, such as hover states and right-click context menus, are possible thanks to the mouse cursor's pinpoint precision, controlled by the wrist and hand's fine motor movements. Designers must account for the distinct affordances and constraints that each input mechanism introduces, ensuring usability across diverse physical contexts.

The physical object determines the broader interaction paradigm, extending beyond simple input mechanics. A speech interface, for example, requires a fully conversational and audio-forward design strategy because it lacks a standard screen or pointer. In addition to addressing environmental challenges such as ambient noise, it must excel at comprehending natural language, delivering clear auditory feedback, and providing gentle recovery paths for misunderstandings. Similarly, a VR controller operating in a simulated 3D space demands an understanding of spatial relationships, depth perception, and natural human movement to generate interactions that feel immersive rather than disorienting. The device's physicality becomes the primary lens through which people users perceive and engage with the digital environment.

The method is defined by the medium. Adapting the interface's presentation and logic to the physical realities of the chosen input device is more critical to successful design than attempting to create a single, universal solution. More than responsive scaling is required; interaction patterns, feedback systems, and error tolerance must be fundamentally rethought depending on whether the user is reaching into a virtual environment, speaking into a microphone, clicking with a mouse, or tapping with a finger. The designer's role is to craft seamless communication between human intent and computer response through the physical device, bridging the gap between the software's abstract logic and the user's tangible, embodied experience.

5.4.2 Environmental Space: Context of Use

The digital interface is always experienced within specific environmental circumstances that significantly shape user engagement; it does not in a vacuum. The surrounding environment determines the conditions in which interactions occur while the physical object dictates how users submit commands. Designers must anticipate and account for a complex matrix of environmental constraints, including lighting, noise levels, social context, physical mobility, and competing attentional demands. For example, a banking application used in a quiet home office functions very differently the same app accessed during rush hour on a crowded, noisy subway. Effective context-aware design must either proactively compensate for or dynamically adapt to environmental variables that influence human perception, attention, and capacity.

Certain design responses are required to address critical environmental conditions. To preserve readability and prevent eye strain, interfaces must adapt to varying lighting contexts, from bright sunlight to dim bedrooms, through high-contrast settings, dark themes, and automated brightness adjustments. The acoustic environment determines whether auditory feedback is effective or whether visual or haptic alternatives should be provided. Likewise, the social context introduces privacy and discretion concerns, making features such as protected screen views and quick-exit buttons essential.

Designs that support one-handed operation, glanceable information, and hands-free alternatives are essential when physical mobility is limited, whether walking, driving, or standing in a crowded area. Likewise, interfaces must manage cognitive load through progressive disclosure, simplified information hierarchies, and intelligent interruption handling in contexts where attention is heavily divided. The overarching principle is clear: interfaces must remain responsive to the environmental circumstances in which they are used, with context defining the constraints that shape effective design.

5.5 The Fourth Dimension – Time

The Dimension of Change and Progress

The Fourth Dimension, Time focuses on the evolution of the user experience through moments, transitions, and durations, Time. It encompasses the dynamic aspects of motion, music, and rhythm that unfold during an interaction, moving beyond static screens. This dimension is essential for transforming a collection of disparate states into a coherent narrative the user can easily comprehend.

The primary goals of time-conscious design are to manage user expectations, provide continuous feedback, and establish a smooth flow. It enables users to understand what is happening now, what has just occurred, and what they can anticipate next, helping them build a clear mental model of the system's behavior.

Ultimately, a sense of competence and control depends heavily on this temporal clarity.

5.5.1 *Animation & Sound*

The use of animation and sound to convey state changes and offer sensory feedback is a key design factor. For example, a menu sliding in from the side offers a subtle animation that seamlessly transitions between two states, avoiding an abrupt or jarring shift. Similarly, pressing a button may produce a gentle "click" sound, serving as immediate, non-visual confirmation that the action has been registered.

5.5.2 *Duration*

The duration of an engagement concerns how time is perceived within an interaction. Designers must consider the length of an action and whether it feels appropriate. When a process cannot be completed instantly, the interface should notify the user, typically through a progress bar or loading animation. By showing that the system is functioning and indicating how long the wait will be, designers prevent confusion and frustration, fostering trust and smoother user experiences.

5.5.3 *Pacing*

Pacing is about giving users control over the flow of time throughout an experience. This includes the ability to pause a video, rewind a tutorial, or skip ahead in a multi-step process. By allowing users to move at their own pace, the design respects individual needs and prevents them from feeling rushed or constrained by the system's predetermined tempo.

5.5.4 *History*

An awareness of history acknowledges that people change their minds and make mistakes. By enabling users to move back and forth in their interaction timeline, features like "Undo" and "Redo" reduce the anxiety caused by permanent, irrevocable actions. This safety net empowers users to explore the interface with greater confidence.

A common example of this dimension is the process of sending an email. The progress indicator "Sending..." provides immediate confirmation that the action is underway. This is followed by a "Message Sent!" notification, which then fades away gracefully after a short duration. The sequence of action, feedback, and resolution is carefully timed to deliver clarity, reassurance, and a satisfying sense of closure.

5.6 The Fifth Dimension – Behavior

The Fifth Dimension, Behaviour, captures the dynamic essence of interaction: the functional and conversational interplay between the user and the product. It transforms the static elements defined by the first four dimensions into a living dialogue that shapes how the product operates and how users achieve their goals. This is the point where design evolves from creating an artifact to orchestrating an experience. For instance, in a banking app, behavior determines whether a transaction can be modified with a simple tap or requires entering a distinct "edit" mode. Likewise, it defines whether dragging a file into a folder feels immediate and responsive or slow and disconnected.

Behaviour consists of two complimentary flows: user actions and system responses. User actions include any method of influencing the interface, such as clicking, swiping, speaking, or gesturing. For example, you might delete a photo on your phone by long-pressing it, swiping left, or tapping the trash icon. System responses encompass the product's intelligent feedback, ranging from immediate functional cues, like a subtle vibration after a successful fingerprint scan, to delayed emotional reinforcements, such as a celebratory burst of confetti after achieving a fitness goal in a health app. Together, these components form the interactive loop that defines the human-system relationship.

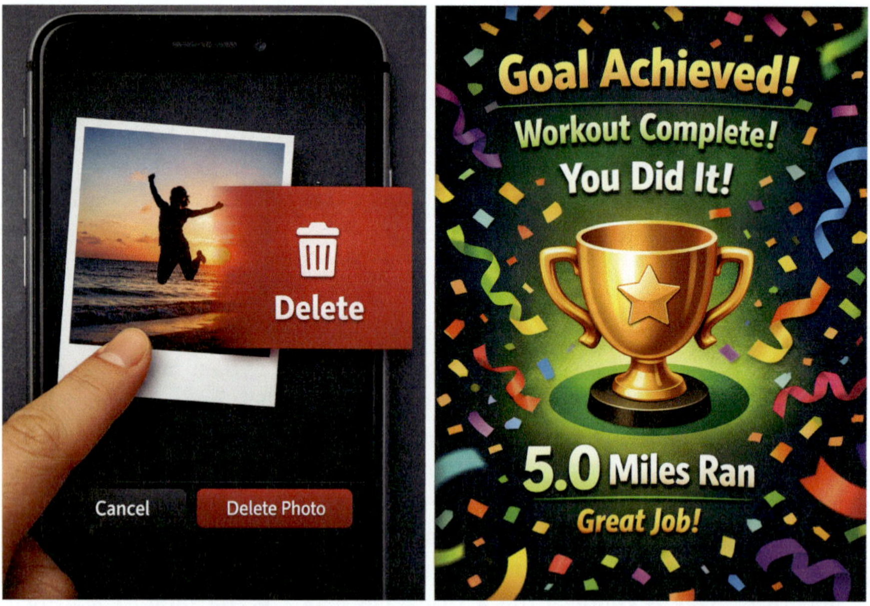

Figure 5.1: The interactive loop between user actions and system reactions defines behavioral design. User inputs trigger intelligent responses ranging from immediate feedback to emotional reinforcement, creating a dynamic dialogue with the product.

This dimension represents the culmination of all preceding design considerations. Words (such as "Reply" and "Forward"), visuals (like the layout of an email client), the physical context (such as using a laptop trackpad), and time (for example, the speed at which an inbox loads) all set the stage, but it is behavior that animates these elements through responsive logic. For instance, in Google Docs, the ability to see another user's cursor move in real time, with their name attached, transforms a static word processor into a collaborative workspace. This dimension converts static design into functional intelligence.

The quality of a product's behavior determines whether users experience it as intuitive and responsive or confusing and frustrating. Well-designed behavior fosters collaboration, for example, when a map application automatically reroutes around traffic and displays the time saved. Poorly designed behavior, on the other hand disrupts the interaction, for instance, when a form deletes all entered data after a single validation error, leaving users confused and disengaged. Ultimately, this dimension is where user trust is earned or eroded with each interaction.

Table 5.9: Behavioral design quality directly impacts user perception.

Well-Designed	**Poorly-Designed**
• Feels intuitive and responsive • Builds user confidence and trust • Encourages continued engagement • Provides clarity and reassurance	• Feels confusing and frustrating • Breaks user trust and flow • Leads to abandonment • Creates anxiety
Example: Maps app reroutes around traffic	*Example:* Form erases all data after one error

Behavior extends beyond basic utility to emotive design. It evaluates not only whether an activity is effective, but also how it feels to perform. The satisfying "pull-to-refresh" bounce in a social media feed, the reassuring autosave icon that pulses before displaying a checkmark in a design tool, or the prominently placed "Sign in with Google" button when creating a new account are all examples of behavioral touches that elevate utilitarian interactions into memorable, valued experiences. A particularly notable example is Gmail's "undo send" option, which provides users with a brief grace period to retract an email, reducing anxiety and increasing confidence.

Information Architecture (IA)	Interaction Design (IxD)
Organizing and labeling websites to support usability.	Designing interactive digital products, environments, systems, and services.
Defining information structure to help users find information.	Defining system behaviors to show how users take actions.
Users, software, existing data, and information representation.	Creating seamless interfaces with essential tools for goal completion.
Researching business and audience needs, analyzing data, organizing and labeling content, and developing website structures.	Performing usability tests, conducting customer interviews, designing interactive layouts, and preparing documents for visual teams.
Layout, navigation, search systems, content structure.	User actions, triggered reactions, task completion.
Transforming complex content into well-organized and understandable information.	Managing the interaction between the application and its users.
Related to the content of the interface.	Related to the flow or transition within the interface.

5.7 Relationship Between IA and Interaction Design

5.8 Principles of Effective Interaction Design

Donald Norman outlines seven fundamental principles of interaction design. These principles work together to create a seamless interaction between users and products, whether a physical object, a website, or a mobile app (Norman Donald, 2013).

5.8.1 Discoverability

Discoverability is the foundational principle that ensures users can immediately understand what actions are possible with a product and how to perform them. It answers the most basic user question: "What can I do here?" This principle is achieved when design makes functions clear, for example, the labeled buttons on a remote control or the visible handles on a door. In software, a well-structured menu makes its options discoverable. A failure of discoverability is illustrated by a hidden door on a blank, smooth wall, where users have no indication that the door exists or how to operate it. The result is confusion and an inability to proceed.

5.8.2 *Feedback*

Feedback is the crucial communication loop between a product and its user. It requires that the product provide clear, immediate, and often continuous information about the results of an action and the current state of the system. Examples include a click sound or haptic vibration on a smartphone, a progress bar during a file download or the familiar "ding" of an arriving elevator. Effective feedback confirms that an input has been received and processed, eliminating uncertainty. The importance of this principle becomes starkly clear when feedback is absent; pressing a button with no response leaves the user wondering whether the action was registered, whether the device is malfunctioning, or whether it is silently processing in the background.

5.8.3 *Conceptual Model*

A Conceptual Model is the simple, clear explanation of how a system works as projected to the user. Good design fosters a consistent and intuitive conceptual model that the user can internalize, giving them a sense of understanding and control. Common examples include the "shopping cart" metaphor on e-commerce sites or the "desktop" with "files" and "folders" on a computer. When this model is broken, for instance, a gear shift that uses a non-standard sequence without a clear diagram, it violates user expectations and leads to errors and frustration.

5.8.4 *Affordances*

Affordances define the relationship between a physical object and a person, indicating how the object can potentially be used. An affordance represents an action possibility; a chair affords sitting, a button affords pressing, and a handle affords pulling. It is important to recognize that affordances suggest possibilities, not instructions. For example, a door handle affords pulling, but it does not explicitly tell the user to pull. This distinction is crucial for understanding the next principle, since the responsibility for communicating specific actions lies with signifiers.

5.8.5 *Signifiers*

Signifiers are perceivable indicators that communicate appropriate behavior to a person. They signal where an affordance can be found and how it should be used. For example, while a handle is an affordance for pulling, a "PULL" sign placed on it serves as the signifier. Other examples include the visual groove around a button, a floppy disk icon to signify "save," or a highlighted path in a mobile app.

Good design employs clear signifiers to draw attention to existing affordances; without them, users may overlook a function entirely.

5.8.6 Mappings

Mappings describe to the relationship between controls and their effects. Good mapping makes this relationship clear and intuitive by leveraging spatial layout or natural cultural associations. A classic example is a stove where the controls are arranged in the same pattern as the burners they operate. Similarly, turning a steering wheel to the left makes the car turn left, and sliding a dimmer switch upward increases brightness. Poor mapping, for instance, a stove with four burners arranged in a square but controls placed in a single row, forces users to guess, leading to errors and inefficiency.

5.8.7 Constraints

Constraints are limitations placed on possible actions to guide the user and make a product easier and safer to use. They work by making incorrect actions impossible or difficult, thereby preventing errors. Constraints can be physical, such as a USB plug that only fits in one orientation. They can also be logical, like a dialog box that prevents selecting "Shut Down" and "Restart" simultaneously. In addition, cultural constraints rely on learned conventions, for example, red for "stop" and green for "go," while semantic constraints rely on meaning, such as the expectation that liquid belongs in a cup, not on a plate.

5.8.8 How They Work Together

These seven principles are not isolated rules but part of a deeply interconnected system. Signifiers make affordances discoverable, while effective mappings and constraints help establish a sound conceptual model. Feedback then reinforces this model by confirming successful actions. When applied together, these principles enable designers to create products that feel natural, minimize user error and frustration, and ultimately provide a pleasurable experience.

5.9 Heuristic Evaluation: Nielsen's Usability Principles

While Norman's principles provide a foundational theory for designing interactions, a complementary set of practical guidelines is necessary to evaluate the quality of a design once it has been created. Heuristic evaluation is a usability inspection method in which experts assess an interface against a set of established principles, or "heuristics." The most enduring and widely adopted of these guidelines are Jakob Nielsen's 10 Usability Heuristics for User Interface Design (Nielsen (1994a)). These heuristics serve as broad guidelines that highlight common usability issues and provide a benchmark for interaction quality. Together, they encompass the core requirements for a usable, learnable, and human-centered interface. The ten heuristics are listed and summarized in Table 5.10.

Table 5.10: Summary of Nielsen's 10 usability heuristics.

S. No.	Heuristic Name	Core Description
1	Visibility of System Status	Keep users informed about what is happening through timely feedback.
2	Match Between System and the Real World	Use familiar language concepts, and conventions that follow real-world logic.
3	User Control and Freedom	Provide clearly marked "emergency exits" to leave unwanted actions; support undo and redo.
4	Consistency and Standards	Ensure users don't have to wonder if different words, actions, or situations mean the same thing; follow platform and industry conventions.
5	Error Prevention	Prevent problems before they occur by eliminating error-prone conditions or presenting confirmation options.
6	Recognition Rather than Recall	Minimize memory load by making elements, actions, and options visible. The user should not have to remember information from one part of the interface to another.
7	Flexibility and Efficiency of Use	Provide shortcuts for experts while allowing customization of frequent actions.
8	Aesthetic and Minimalist Design	Avoid irrelevant or rarely needed information; keep interfaces clear and focused.
9	Help Users Recognize, Diagnose, and Recover from Errors	Use plain language in error messages, indicate the problem clearly, and suggest constructive solutions.
10	Help and Documentation	Even if a system should be usable without documentation, provide easy-to-search, task-focused help when necessary.

5.9.1 Relationship to Foundational Principles

Nielsen's heuristics are not a replacement for the principles of Interaction Design (IxD) or Norman's design principles; rather, they operationalize those principles into a set of evaluative criteria. There is significant synergy and overlap, as shown in Table 5.11. For instance, Norman's principle of **Feedback** is directly embodied in Heuristic 1 (*Visibility of System Status*). Likewise, his concepts of **Affordances** and **Signifiers** are essential for achieving Heuristic 2 (*Match Between System and the Real World*) and Heuristic 6 (*Recognition Rather than Recall*).

Table 5.11: Synergy between Nielsen's heuristics and foundational design principles.

Nielsen's Heuristic	**Connection to IxD/Norman's Principles**
Visibility of System Status	Implements Norman's **Feedback** principle; tied to the Fourth Dimension (**Time**).
Match Between System and the Real World	Relies **Affordances** and **Signifiers**; supports the First Dimension (**Words**: Clarity & Simplicity).
User Control and Freedom	Enables user-centric behavior described in the Fifth Dimension (**Behavior**), supporting exploration and error recovery.
Consistency and Standards	Echoes the First Dimension (**Words**: **Consistency**) and strengthens the Conceptual Model.
Error Prevention	Applies Norman's **Constraints** and **Mappings**, proactively eliminating slips and mistakes.
Recognition Rather than Recall	Supported by clear **Signifiers** and effective **Visual Representations** (Second Dimension).
Flexibility and Efficiency of Use	Enhances the **Behavior** dimension by accommodating varied expertise and personalization.
Aesthetic and Minimalist Design	Aligns with the Second Dimension (**Visual Representations**) to create focused, purposeful interfaces.
Error Recovery	Completes the feedback loop from Heuristic 1, using clear language (**Words**) to guide users from problems to solutions.
Help and Documentation	Provides a final support layer within the **Behavior** dimension, acknowledging that even well-designed systems may require explanation for complex tasks.

5.9.2 Application in the Design Process

Heuristic evaluation is typically employed as a discount usability method during the iterative design process. Once a prototype or existing product is available, evaluators, ideally three to five usability experts, independently examine the interface and assess its compliance with the ten heuristics. The identified violations are then aggregated and prioritized by severity. This method is highly efficient for uncovering a significant proportion of usability issues before conducting more resource-intensive user testing.

In conclusion, Nielsen's 10 Usability Heuristics provide a vital, pragmatic lens through which to critique and improve interaction design. They translate the theoretical goals of the Five Dimensions and Norman's principles into a concrete checklist, ensuring that the final product is not only conceptually sound but also practically usable, efficient, and satisfying for the end user.

5.10 Conclusion/Summary of Interaction Design

Interaction design is the discipline that shapes how people interact with and experience digital products. It is built on a comprehensive framework known as the Five Dimensions: precise word choice for clear communication, thoughtful visual representations for intuitive perception, consideration of the physical context of devices and environments, time management through feedback and pacing, and the definition of intelligent system behavior. These dimensions are guided by Don Norman's core concepts, such as discoverability, feedback, and affordances, which explain why certain interactions feel natural. Jakob Nielsen's 10 Usability Heuristics provide an essential checklist for evaluation, emphasizing visibility, error prevention, and user control. Ultimately, interaction design collaborates with information architecture to produce coherent, efficient, and fulfilling digital experiences that help users achieve their goals. Information architecture provides the ordered framework, while interaction design defines the responsive, engaging pathways.

Chapter 6

Visual Design and Branding

The goal is to convey interactions and behaviors through a logical visual language. Beyond simple aesthetics, principles like color, font, spacing, and iconography serve as fundamental tools that enhance a product's sensory quality, guide attention, and make interactions noticeable. This section examines both the theoretical and practical frameworks of branding and visual design, emphasizing their crucial role in creating cohesive and successful user experiences. It explores how brand perception and identity are shaped by visual elements such as color, typography, imagery, and layout. Key topics include the psychology of design, the necessity of visual consistency, and the role of branding in fostering user loyalty and trust. Additionally, it highlights how accessibility and visual design work together to ensure inclusivity for diverse user groups. To demonstrate practical applications, case studies and best practices are presented, offering readers with specific insights into developing aesthetically pleasing and authentic brand identities.

6.1 Principles of Visual Design

Visual design principles provide a scientific and psychological foundation for creating interfaces that are not only aesthetically pleasing but also highly usable. By understanding how the human eye and brain perceive visual information, designers can craft layouts that guide users intuitively, reduce cognitive load, and strengthen the overall user experience. Gordon, K. (2020) identifies five visual design principles that significantly influence user experience (UX).

DOI: 10.1201/9781003715764-6

6.1.1 The Principle of Scale

The Principle of Scale explains how relative size is strategically used in visual composition to impose structural organization, indicate significance, and establish hierarchy. Rooted in psychophysics, it recognizes that larger visual elements are inherently perceived by the human brain as more significant and authoritative. In interface design, this correlation between perceived worth and size is not only visually appealing but also serves as a key cognitive mechanism for prioritizing information.

Scale serves as a direct modulator of visual salience, the ability of an element to draw pre-attentive processing. Research in visual cognition shows that larger stimuli trigger stronger neural responses in the visual cortex, leading to quicker detection times and improved memorability. In practice, scale is one of the most effective tools for managing discoverability, ensuring that crucial interface elements, such as important data, core actions, and significant content, capture users' attention instantaneously.

Effective application necessitates systematic constraints rather than uncontrolled variance. Designers should design a typographic scale, defined as a succession of sizes linked to a base unit (e.g., 16px for body text) and multiplied consistently. This produces a hierarchical sequence (e.g., 12px, 16px, 24px, 32px, 48px) with distinct steps between levels of importance.

A well-structured scale has three key characteristics:

- Limit variance: Restrict size options to three tiers (small, medium, large) within any single view.
- Consistent linkages: Maintain proportional ratios across all scalable elements.
- Contextual adaptation: Adjust sizes based on viewport dimensions and viewing distance.

Wayfinding systems use scale as an orienting aid in multi-level parking facilities. Directional or instructional text is typically three to five times smaller than zone identification signs ("Zone H"). By leveraging spatial memory encoding, this extreme scaling enables users to quickly locate and remember their parking position, even in visually complex environments.

When scale is applied effectively, it eliminates unnecessary visual competition and reduces cognitive load, enabling users to grasp interface hierarchies without conscious effort. This leads to quantifiable performance improvements, such as quicker decision-making (information-finding tasks show 40–60% reduction in completion time), greater accuracy in distinguishing primary from secondary actions, and increased satisfaction as users perceive scaled interfaces to be more professional, clear, and trustworthy.

Common implementation errors include:

- Scale inflation: Overusing large elements diminishes contrast and collapses hierarchy.
- Inconsistent progression: Arbitrary size choices create visual noise rather than clear structure.
- Accessibility neglect: Failure to maintain minimum contrast ratios between scaled elements and their backgrounds.

Thus, the Principle of Scale is more than just a stylistic choice; it is a key information-architectural technique. When carefully calibrated, it converts random visual arrangements into coherent hierarchical structures aligned with human perceptual capacities, resulting in interfaces that feel intuitive rather than prescriptive.

6.1.2 The Principle of Visual Hierarchy

Imagine walking into a library where every book is the same size, has the same color cover, and is spaced at identical intervals across endless shelves. You would wander for hours, scanning spines and paralyzed by indecision. Now imagine that same library with clear section signage, prominent displays, and best-selling volumes facing forward. Suddenly, anyone can find what they need in minutes. This is the power of visual hierarchy, the difference between a tedious maze and an intuitive path. Visual hierarchy illustrates the psychological design of digital spaces: how the human brain knows where to look first without instruction, why a button feels more important than a link, and why some programs feel effortless while others feel like work.

When viewing a screen, the brain is not perceiving pixels; it is executing a sophisticated pattern-recognition process refined over millennia. Before conscious thought begins, the visual cortex has already

- Identified the most significant element (size detection: "That's important!").
- Noticed what is different (contrast processing: "That stands out!")
- Grouped related items (pattern recognition: "These belong together!")
- Tracked natural lines (flow detection: "This leads somewhere!")

Visual hierarchy works because it leverages the brain's native language of perception. It does not require conscious thought; rather, it aligns with how individuals naturally process visual information.

Consider the Uber vs. Dropbox comparison. Uber exemplifies effective visual hierarchy: when users launch the app, their eyes instinctively focus on the "Where to?" field within 200 milliseconds, thanks to its center-top placement and strong visual contrast. The contextual map appears as a secondary element, smaller and positioned below, while recent locations are displayed in a lighter, less obtrusive font. Uber's design succeeds because it directly addresses the first question users have when opening the app, making the core task of booking a ride not just obvious but unavoidable. By contrast, early versions of Dropbox struggled with hierarchy. Files and folders were presented in a plain spreadsheet-style format, with minimal visual differentiation between categories. To locate a file, users had to scan left to right, carefully read text labels, and make deliberate comparisons at each step. This imposed a heavy cognitive load. Rather than efficiently managing files, users felt as though they were deciphering hieroglyphics, which increased both the time and mental effort required for basic tasks.

Visual hierarchy can be understood as a continuum ranging from disruptive to seamless.

- Level 0 – Visual chaos: Reminiscent of early 1990s websites, where every element competes for attention, shouting "LOOK AT ME!" without providing a clear starting point. Users typically abandon such interfaces almost immediately.
- Level 1 – Basic organization: Seen in functional but uninspiring enterprise software, where items are categorised but locating information still feels laborious and time-consuming.
- Level 2 – Clear flow: Exemplified by well-designed news sites; where essential content is obvious and the reading path that feels natural and pleasant, though not particularly memorable.
- Level 3 – Invisible guidance: Demonstrated by platforms such as Airbnb, Uber, and Apple, where users achieve their objectives effortlessly. The design anticipates their needs, and the experience feels "right," even if the underlying reasons remain unnoticed.

Several common pitfalls might jeopardise a successful hierarchy. Hierarchy overload occurs when too many elements are presented as equally significant, leaving none truly prominent, similar to a homepage with a dozen components blinking, animating, and competing for attention simultaneously. Another risk arises when designers prioritize aesthetics over function, favoring "clean looks" at the expense of clarity. For instance, light gray text on a white background may appear minimalist, but it causes visual strain, resulting in what could be described as tyranny for tired eyes. Finally, inconsistent regulations pose an additional barrier. When equivalent objects have receive graphic treatments without a clear justification, forcing users to guess whether a blue button means "Save" or "Delete."

Visual hierarchy extends far beyond aesthetics, delivering both practical and emotional benefits. It significantly improves efficiency, with well-structured hierarchy reducing decision-making time by up to 80%, enabling users to locate what they need much faster. It also enhances satisfaction, as clear interfaces inspire confidence, while complex ones foster distrust. From an accessibility perspective, strong hierarchy supports all users, particularly those with attention challenges, low vision, or cognitive disabilities. The financial impact is equally notable: studies show that even minor delays can result in substantial losses, whereas effectively reduces cognitive latency. Finally, hierarchy shapes emotional connection. Frustration breeds resentment, while ease fosters trust and loyalty.

A realistic framework can guide the creation of an effective visual hierarchy. The process begins by defining the single most critical action users must take in a given context. That primary action should then be made unmistakable through the strategic use of size, contrast, and positioning. All other elements should be logically organized, with items of comparable importance receiving consistent visual treatment. Clear levels must be established–typically: Major: the primary action, Secondary: supporting alternatives, and Tertiary: additional details. Finally, the design must pass the "5-second test": can someone glance at the interface and instantly know what to do?

The most successful visual hierarchy goes unnoticed, much like a skilled host who guides guests without drawing attention to the effort. It clarifies what is significant, connects related parts, and fosters a sense of comfort and clarity. When implemented effectively, users do not praise the design itself; instead, they accomplish their goals and leave with a positive impression of the experience. Ultimately, the greatest compliment a design can receive is not "This looks beautiful," but rather "This just makes sense." This underscores the critical idea that visual hierarchy is not primarily about aesthetics, but about reducing cognitive effort. In a world saturated with digital distractions, the most valuable gift designers can offer is less confusion, not more features.

6.1.3 The Principle of Balance

The uniform distribution of visual weight in a composition is known as balance. An element's ability to attract attention determines its visual weight, a perceptual characteristic influenced by factors such as size, color, contrast, intricacy, and placement. Larger, darker, denser, or more detailed objects naturally feel "heavier." Whether symmetrical, asymmetrical, or radial, a balanced composition achieves equilibrium and conveys an innate sense of harmony, stability, and order. Conversely, an uneven layout often feels uncomfortable and unprofessional, eroding user confidence and detracting from the content.

Designers employ three major types of balance, each creating a unique psychological effect:

- Symmetrical balance: Achieved by mirroring elements exactly or nearly identically across a central axis. This formal, ordered design conveys peace, stability, and dependability, often associated with institutions and conventional settings.
- Asymmetrical balance: Created by arranging different elements with equal visual weight on each side of the axis, for example, a large image balanced by a cluster of smaller text blocks, or a bold color offset by negative space. This approach feels lively, modern, and engaging, suggesting energy and movement.
- Radial balance: Formed by organizing elements around a central focal point that radiates outward. While visually striking and unifying, radial balance is less common in interface design, as it can disrupt conventional layout patterns and appear gimmicky if not applied carefully.

The effect of balance on user experience is often subconscious. A well-balanced design seems resolved, allowing users to focus their cognitive effort on tasks rather than deciphering layout. However, imbalance introduces subtle tension, diminishing perceived professionalism and trust. A stable layout demonstrates skill and intentionality, which fosters engagement and confidence.

Examples of balance in action include: Symmetrical balance: The job-search platform The Hub conveys trust and formality, Asymmetrical balance: Nike's website conveys athletic dynamism and energy, and Radial balance: Spotify's "Wrapped" campaign creates a personalized, joyful emphasis.

6.1.4 The Principle of Contrast

Contrast is a foundational design principle defined by the strategic juxtaposition of visually dissimilar elements. By intentionally varying properties like color, size, or shape, designers signal that certain elements are distinct from others. This distinction is not merely aesthetic; it is one of the most powerful tools for creating clear signifiers within an interface. Contrast communicates to the user, "These things are not the same," making it essential for distinguishing interactive elements from static content, highlighting errors, establishing a visual hierarchy, and categorizing information effectively.

Although often first associated with color, such as a red "Delete" button standing out against a neutral background, contrast is a versatile tool that operates across multiple channels. Size contrast: A large, prominent button is immediately perceived as more important than a small text link. Shape contrast: Differentiating a rounded, pill-shaped primary button from a rectangular text

(a)

(b)

(c)

Figure 6.1: (a) Symmetrical (Formal) Balance, (b) Asymmetrical (Dynamic) Balance, (c) Radial (Circular) Balance.

input field guides user interaction. Typographic contrast: Using bold font weight for a headline against regular body text establishes structure and directs the reader's eye through content.

A critical and non-negotiable application of contrast lies in the realm of accessibility. The contrast ratio between text and its background is essential for ensuring legibility for all users, including those with visual impairments like low vision or color blindness. While low-contrast text, such as light gray on a white background, may appear stylish, it creates a significant barrier to usability, rendering information difficult or even impossible to read for a large portion of the population. To prevent this, the use of automated color-contrast checkers during the design process is an indispensable practice for creating inclusive and compliant digital products.

The iOS Reminders app provides a clear example of effective, functional contrast. When a user attempts to delete a list, the "Delete List" option is displayed in a bright, high-contrast red. This color choice immediately distinguishes the action apart from neutral options such as "Cancel" or "Share List." The visual contrast acts as a universal warning, signaling that the function is different, destructive, and requires deliberate consideration.

In contrast, the packaging for Greenhouse Juice Co. serves as a counter-example where aesthetic choices compromise legibility. The label color on their bottles often provides insufficient contrast against the light-colored juices inside. This makes critical information, such as the flavor name or ingredients, difficult and straining to read. This failure in contrast forces the user to work to decipher basic information, undermining the user experience and demonstrating how a lack of functional contrast can hinder the primary purpose of a design, which in this case is to communicate product details clearly and effortlessly.

6.1.5 The Gestalt Principles

Collectively, these five visual-design principles form the bedrock of effective and humane digital experiences. They are not arbitrary rules of aesthetics but are rooted in the very way human perception and cognition work. By strategically applying visual hierarchy, balance, contrast, and the principles of Gestalt, designers move beyond mere decoration to create interfaces that communicate, guide, and function with clarity and purpose. This disciplined approach transforms a chaotic assembly of pixels into a coherent, self-evident system that users can understand and use intuitively.

The most direct impact of these principles is a dramatic increase in usability. A clear visual hierarchy tells users where to look first, guiding them effortlessly through content and actions. Logical groupings established by Gestalt principles like proximity and similarity make complex information easy to parse. Strong contrast ensures that interactive elements are immediately distinguishable from static ones. The result is an interface that is faster to scan, easier to navigate, and more efficient to use, leading directly to higher task-completion rates and reduced user frustration.

Beyond pure functionality, these principles are powerful tools for provoking positive emotion and delight. A balanced composition feels stable and professional, subconsciously building user trust. A harmonious and aesthetically pleasing design, achieved through thoughtful application of these laws, elicits a favorable emotional response. This is captured by the aesthetic-usability effect, where users are more forgiving of minor usability issues and report a more satisfying experience when they find an interface visually appealing.

The consistent application of these principles is fundamental to building a strong and trustworthy brand perception. A cohesive visual system, where hierarchy, balance, and contrast are used reliably, tells a cohesive brand story. It signals competence, care, and attention to detail, making a product feel more professional and reliable. This fosters user confidence and loyalty, as people are naturally drawn to and prefer to use systems that feel coherent, predictable, and designed with their needs in mind.

These perceptual concepts explain the why of effective visual communication. To put them into practice, designers use a set of concrete, defining materials known as the basic elements of a visual identity. These aspects, including the logo, color palette, typography, artwork, and layout rules, transform abstract concepts into a consistent and recognizable brand language.

6.2 The Core Elements of a Visual Identity

A visual identity is the collection of elements a company uses to express its personality, essence, and values to the world. It goes beyond a simple logo to form a comprehensive system that ensures consistency across every touchpoint. This consistency makes a brand instantly recognizable, builds trust, and fosters a strong connection with its audience. At its core, a visual identity answers the question: "What do we look like?", and its foundational elements serve as the building blocks of that answer.

6.2.1 Logo

The logo is the cornerstone of a brand's visual identity, serving as its primary graphic symbol and the most concise visual representation of the brand's essence. It is a distinctive mark designed for instant recognition, representing the business across all touchpoints, from digital applications to physical products. A well-designed logo is more than just an attractive image; it is a strategic asset that encapsulates a company's values, mission, and personality in a single, memorable unit. Its fundamental role is to identify, not to explain, acting as the visual shorthand for the entire brand. Logos are not one-size-fits-all; they exist in several distinct types, each with unique strengths and applications (Stevens, E., 2023).

- Wordmark or Logotype: This consists of the company name itself, stylized with custom typography. It is ideal for businesses with distinctive, short names, as it helps build strong name recognition. Well-known examples include Google and Coca-Cola (Figure 6.2).

Figure 6.2: Coca-Cola and Google logo.

- Lettermark (or Monogram): This type of logo simplifies a longer business name into its initials, creating a sleek, professional symbol that is highly versatile. Well-known examples include IBM and HBO, both of which use lettermarks effectively to achieve instant recognition.

Figure 6.3: IBM and HBO logo.

- Pictorial Mark: This type of logo uses a literal, iconic image to represent the brand, such as Apple's apple or Twitter's bird. Pictorial marks enable strong cross-linguistic recognition, making them effective symbols in diverse global contexts.

Figure 6.4: Apple and Twitter logo.

- Abstract Mark: This type of logo employs a unique geometric form to express a brand's concept or emotion rather than a literal image.

Examples include the Nike Swoosh, which conveys dynamic energy, and the Pepsi globe, which symbolizes global unity.

Figure 6.5: Nike and Pepsi logo.

- Combination Mark: This type of logo integrates both a symbol, whether pictorial or abstract, and the company name text, locking them together into a single unit. Brands such as Adidas and Burger King use combination marks to build graphic recognition while simultaneously reinforcing the brand name (Figure 6.5).

Figure 6.6: Addidas and Burger King logo.

- Emblem: This type of logo frames the company name within a symbol or badge, creating a classic, traditional, and often robust feel. Emblems are strongly associated with authority and heritage, as exemplified by Stella Artois and Harley-Davidson.

6.2.2 Color Palette

Colour is the most impactful and emotional tool in a brand's visual identity. It operates at a pre-conscious level, triggering perception, shaping psychological responses, and forming visceral associations before any content is absorbed. A deliberately designed color system is therefore more than just visually appealing,

Figure 6.7: Stella Artois and Harley-Davidson logo.

it serves as a functional foundation for driving awareness, defining brand personality, and influencing user behavior across all touchpoints.

6.2.2.1 The Strategic Architecture of Brand Color

Effective brand color systems are built with intentional hierarchy and function:

- **Primary Color:** The dominant brand identifier (e.g., Coca-Cola red, Tiffany blue). This hue becomes synonymous with the brand itself.
- **Secondary Colors:** Complementary colors that support the primary color, used for visual variety, backgrounds, or to denote distinguish product lines or sections.
- **Neutral Colors:** The structural foundation (white, black, gray, brown) applied to text, backgrounds, and core UI elements to ensure legibility and balance.
- **Accent Color:** A high-contrast hue used sparingly to draw attention to critical interactive elements, notifications, or calls-to-action.

This hierarchical architecture ensures consistency while providing the flexibility for diverse applications, from digital interfaces to physical merchandise.

6.2.2.2 Color Theory for Brand Application

To build a cohesive color system, designers manipulate three core properties of color:

- **Hue:** The color family itself (e.g., red, blue).
- **Saturation:** The intensity or purity of the color, from vivid to muted.
- **Value:** The relative lightness or darkness of a color.

Adjusting these properties produces the variations needed for a complete palette. Mixing a hue with white creates a **tint** (lighter, softer), which often associated with modern, calm, or gentle mood. Adding black results in a darker, richer shade, linked to sophistication, depth, or seriousness. Introducing gray yields a muted, more complex tone, which conveys elegance and feels less aggressive.

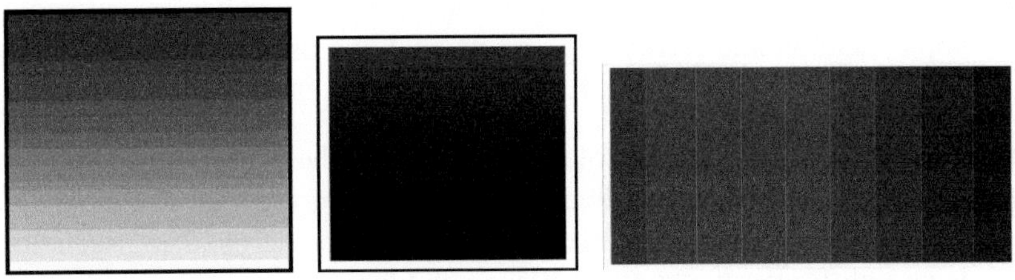

(a) (b) (c)

Figure 6.8: Variations in color value: (a) Tints (adding white), (b) Shades (adding black), and (c) Tones (adding gray) of a base hue.

Colors are perceptually categorized as **warm** (reds, oranges, yellows) or **cool** (blues, greens, purples). Warm colors are *advancing*, they appear closer, stimulate feelings of energy, passion, and urgency. Cool colors are *receding*, they appear farther away, evoking calm, trust, and professionalism. This spatial and psychological effect is fundamental to establishing visual hierarchy and emotional tone.

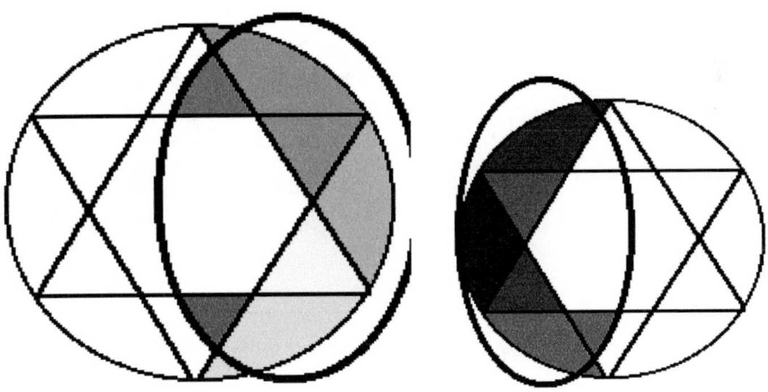

(a) (b)

Figure 6.9: Color temperature: (a) Warm colors (reds, oranges, yellows) and (b) Cool colors (blues, greens, purples).

6.2.2.3 Color Schemes: Strategic Combinations for Brand Goals

These properties are combined into structured **color schemes**, each suited to different brand objectives:

- **Monochromatic:** Uses tints, tones, and shades of a single hue. This scheme creates maximum harmony and cohesion, projecting sophistication and clarity (e.g., a financial app using a range of blues to communicate stability and trust).
- **Complementary:** Pairs colors opposite on the wheel (e.g., blue and orange). This scheme delivers maximum contrast and vibrancy, ideal for grabbing attention and conveying dynamic energy. The psychology is straightforward: a brand can leverage blue's trustworthiness alongside orange's friendliness and creativity (e.g., PayPal's blue and orange).
- **Analogous:** Uses three to five adjacent colors (e.g., yellow, yellow-green, green). This scheme produces serene, low-contrast harmony, often evoking natural, organic, or tranquil brand associations (e.g., health or wellness brands).
- **Neutral-Base with Accent:** Relies primarily on neutrals with a strategic pop of color. This conveys elegance and timelessness while allowing the accent color to command precise attention, for example, a red "Buy Now" button on a minimalist site.

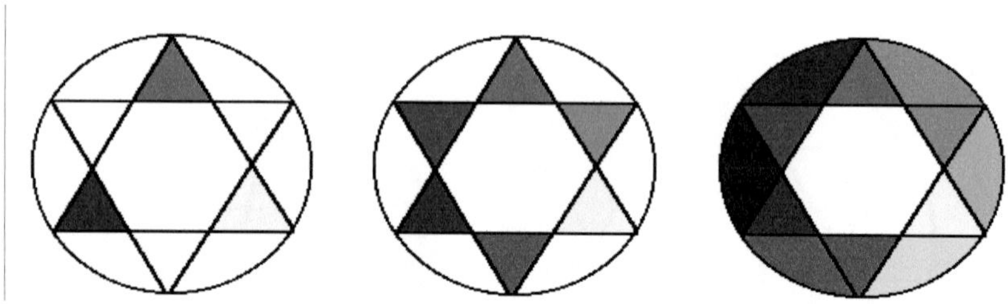

(a) (b) (c)

Figure 6.10: Color wheel fundamentals: (a) Primary colors, (b) Secondary colors, and (c) Tertiary colors.

Neutral colors play a crucial balancing role in all schemes:

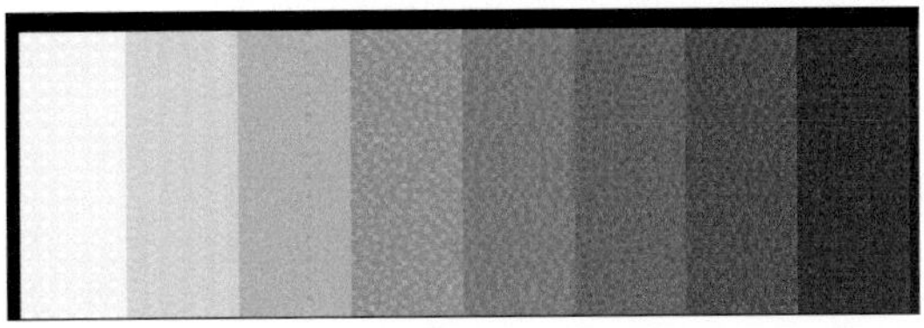

Figure 6.11: Neutral colors (black, white, gray, brown) provide essential structural balance in color systems.

6.2.2.4 Psychology, Context, and Accessibility

While general color psychology offers a starting point, red for excitement, blue for trust, green for growth, its application is nuanced and never absolute. **Context dictates meaning**: a red heart icon conveys love, while a red alert triangle signals danger. **Cultural interpretations also vary significantly**; for example, white represents purity in some cultures but mourning in others. This variability underscores the importance of research and sensitivity.

Most critically, color must serve **accessibility**. Ensuring sufficient contrast between text and background is a non-negotiable requirement for users with low vision. Color should never be the sole means of conveying information (e.g., indicating a "required field" only with red), so that color-blind users are not excluded. Adherence to standards like the Web Content Accessibility Guidelines (WCAG) is essential for achieving inclusive design.

6.2.2.5 Process: Building a Cohesive Brand Palette

Anchor in Brand Attributes: Begin with the brand's core adjectives (e.g., "reliable, innovative, approachable"). For instance, a tech brand might anchor its palette in a trustworthy blue, accented with an innovative violet.

Analyze the Competitive Landscape: Select colors that ensure distinctiveness while remaining appropriate for the industry.

Define the System Hierarchy: Formally designate primary, secondary, neutral, and accent colors, with explicit use cases for each.

Test for Versatility and Compliance: Confirm that the palette functions across all required contexts (e.g., dark mode, print) and meets accessibility contrast ratios.

Document Rigorously: Specify exact color values for all mediums, HEX/RGB for digital and CMYK/Pantone for print, within a brand style guide.

In essence, a brand's color palette is a strategic communication system. By applying color theory with an understanding of psychology, context, and inclusivity, designers transform abstract hues into a powerful, functional asset that guides perception, directs behavior, and cements brand identity.

6.2.3 Typography

Typography is the visual discipline of structuring written language. Its role extends beyond basic legibility, functioning as the primary conduit through which a message's tone, authority, and organizational logic are communicated at a pre-conscious level (Kahn & Lenk, 1998). Even before content is analytically processed, typographic choices establish the perceptual framework that shapes how information is received and interpreted.

6.2.3.1 Goals of Typographic Design

The strategic application of typography serves three interrelated objectives that collectively shape communicative efficacy and user experience.

First, typography establishes perceptual framing. Typeface selection fundamentally influences initial user perception through deeply ingrained associations. For instance, a legal brief rendered in a casual script font would undermine its authority, while a festive invitation set in a formal serif such as Times New Roman would appear incongruously rigid. These responses are not arbitrary; they stem from typographic conventions in which serif typefaces signal tradition and reliability, sans-serif fonts convey modernity and clarity, and script styles suggest elegance or creativity.

Second, typography facilitates cognitive engagement. Effective typography functions as an invisible guide, making the reading process both effortless and compelling. It draws attention through deliberate visual treatments, such as an impactful headline or refined page composition, and sustains engagement by removing barriers to comprehension. This is achieved through optimal legibility, a logical visual hierarchy, and coherent structure that prevent reader fatigue and support sustained interaction with content.

Third, and most fundamentally, typography enables efficient information transmission. It functions as a delivery system that optimizes how users access, process, and retain information. This efficiency manifests in several ways: it allows users to navigate content quickly to locate relevant details; it clarifies conceptual relationships and relative importance through visual differentiation; and it enhances memory retention by presenting information in logically organized structures. These capabilities are achieved through the synergistic application of legibility standards, clear hierarchical signaling, and consistent alignment, enabling users to discern primary content and document architecture within seconds of visual exposure.

Furthermore, typography serves critical organizational functions. At the macro level, it establishes the overall aesthetic character and usability of a communication medium. At the micro level, it employs deliberate stylistic treatments, such as distinctive pull-quotes or title formatting, to create points of visual interest without disrupting coherence. Most importantly, typography creates systematic relationships through consistent styling of equivalent elements. When all first-level headings share identical visual properties, or all captions maintain uniform formatting, typography constructs a visual language that implicitly communicates categorical relationships, signaling to the reader, "These elements represent the same class of information."

6.2.3.2 Design Principles for Typography: The Four Pillars

These four principles are the fundamental tools for achieving the goals outlined above.

- Legibility: The non-negotiable foundation. If text is difficult to read, all other design efforts are wasted. Legibility ensures the message is transmitted without interference.
- Similarity & Alignment: The principles of organization. They impose order out of chaos by grouping related elements and creating a clean, intentional visual structure.
- Uniformity/Consistency: The principle of reinforcement. Consistency produces a predictable and professional experience, builds trust and strengthens the document's structure by repeating visual patterns.
- Contrast & Hierarchy: The principles of differentiation. They generate visual energy and establish an order of importance, guiding the reader's eye to what matters most.

Legibility

Legibility represents the scientific and artistic optimization of textual decoding. It encompasses multiple interdependent factors that collectively determine how efficiently the human visual system can process written information.

Legibility and font families are historically and functionally intertwined. Serif typefaces, defined by short terminal strokes at the extremities of character limbs, have traditionally enhanced print readability through several techniques. Serifs create subtle horizontal cues that guide the eye across, lines of text which is particularly valuable in long-form reading environments such as books and magazines. Additionally, the contrast between thick and thin strokes in many serif designs produces more distinct letter shapes, enabling quick differentiation between similar glyphs, for example, the capital 'I', lowercase 'l', and numeral '1'.

Sans-serif typefaces, which lack these terminal strokes, gained popularity in digital environments due to technological constraints. Early display systems with low resolution (usually 72–96 pixels per inch) rendered serif details poorly, producing visual artifacts that reduced legibility. Sans-serif fonts, with their uniform stroke weights and streamlined forms, remained clear despite these limitations. Although modern high-resolution displays have reduced this disparity, sans-serif typefaces are still preferred for small text sizes and low-resolution applications where retaining detail is challenging.

Body text sizing requires consideration of both physiological and contextual factors. Presbyopia, the age-related decline in near-focus ability, necessitates larger text sizes for older audiences, with research suggesting optimal sizes increase from approximately 10-point for young adults to 12-point or more for readers over 65. Environmental conditions further influence sizing decisions: stable, well-lit environments permit smaller text, while variable lighting and mobile contexts typically demand larger sizes to maintain readability. Paradoxically, excessive text enlargement can impair legibility by disrupting typographic color, the overall gray value created by text density, and interfering with the rhythmic eye movements essential for fluent reading. Text blocks set substantially larger than conventional body sizes (generally exceeding 16-point for extended content) produce overly light tonal values, forcing word-by-word processing rather than phrase recognition.

Spacing forms a vital triangle of interconnected characteristics that directly influence legibility. Letter-spacing (tracking) necessitates careful calibration: insufficient spacing leads glyphs to visually merge, obscuring word structures; excessive spacing fragments words into separate character sequences, forcing cognitive reassembly. Word-spacing consistency is especially critical in justified text alignment, where irregular gaps create distracting "rivers" of white space that disrupt horizontal reading flow. Line spacing (leading) facilitates vertical navigation: insufficient spacing produces line-skipping errors during return sweeps, whereas excessive spacing breaks the visual connection between lines, impeding rhythmic reading.

Alignment strategies differentially affect reading efficiency. Left-aligned (ragged-right) text offers maximum legibility through consistent line-start predictability and natural word-spacing patterns. Its irregular right margin introduces textural variation that can enhance approachability. Justified alignment produces formal, uniform text blocks but compromises legibility through forced adjustments to word and letter spacing, particularly problematic in narrow columns where spacing irregularities become more pronounced. Centered and right-aligned text create variable starting points that increase cognitive load during line location, rendering them unsuitable for extended reading. However, they remain effective for short decorative elements.

Similarity and Alignment

The intentional alignment of elements creates implicit visual structures that convey organizational linkages. When headings, body text, and captions are consistently aligned along invisible vertical axes, they form a perceptual group that signals their membership in a single content system. Edward Tufte described this as "visual parallelism," a design principle that reduces cognitive strain by establishing predictable spatial relationships. The resulting sense of order and coherence arises not from explicit visual connectors, but from the subconscious recognition of aligned edges as markers of conceptual association.

Uniformity and Font Selection

Disciplined font selection exemplifies strategic restraint. Excessive font variety creates a visual cacophony, akin to conflicting auditory signals, that undermines hierarchy and complicates information architecture. A single-font approach (concordance) achieves maximum harmony and sophistication by generating contrast through variations in size, weight, and spacing within the same type family. The classic two-font technique strikes a balance between distinction and coherence, often pairing a serif and a sans-serif to establish clear hierarchical differentiation while maintaining visual consistency.

Font pairing schemes produce diverse perceptual effects. Effective contrast combinations, or example serif headlines and sans-serif body text, leverage fundamental structural differences to create deliberate, intelligible hierarchy. Conversely, conflict arises from pairings lacking sufficient distinctiveness, such as two serif fonts with subtle but noticeable differences in x-height, stroke contrast, or character width. These combinations generate visual tension that appears accidental rather than intentional, confusing rather than clarifying information organization.

Contrast and Spacing Manipulation

Typography employs spatial manipulation at multiple scales to establish hierarchy and emphasis. At the micro-typographic level, tracking adjustments alter inter-character spacing for expressive purposes. Body text typically retains default tracking optimized for small-size readability, whereas display type (headlines, titles) permits controlled expansion or compression. Wide tracking conveys openness and formality, making it suitable for prestigious contexts; tight tracking generates density and impact but requires careful monitoring to preserve character recognition. These modifications operate within the broader framework of typographic color, the overall gray value produced by text density, which must remain balanced across all sections of a page to sustain visual harmony.

Baseline shift techniques introduce deliberate irregularity into text lines. The initial cap (drop cap) is a conventional device that provides visual emphasis and creates entry points into text blocks. More expressive approaches, such as randomized baseline displacement ("jittery text"), generate dynamic, energetic effects but significantly compromise legibility, restricting their use to contexts where visual expression outweighs information transfer.

Hierarchy and Information Architecture

Visual hierarchy is the structural representation of information architecture in typographic form. It provides a perceptual framework for answering basic reader questions about content organization, significance relationships, and navigational pathways. A document without a defined hierarchy appears as an undifferentiated text mass, requiring methodical decoding rather than intuitive comprehension.

Hierarchies are implemented through a set of interdependent variables. Size establishes primary differentiation through proportionate scaling. Weight (ranging from light to black) introduces secondary distinctions within size groups. Color, when applied methodically, produces both functional contrast and emotional resonance. Spacing, the "air" surrounding objects, signals grouping and sectional relationships through proximity and separation. Position within the layout grid conveys implicit importance, guided by cultural reading standards (e.g., top/center emphasis in Western contexts).

Consistency transforms discrete typographic decisions into coherent systems. When stylistic standards dictate that all second-level headers share the same specifications (e.g., 20px size, bold weight, 30px preceding space), predictable patterns emerge that users instinctively internalize. This systematic approach reduces cognitive strain, accelerates navigation, and enhances perceived professionalism by demonstrating attention to detail. The resulting typographic system serves as an unobtrusive interface, guiding users through content with minimal conscious effort. It embodies what information designer Richard Saul Wurman described as "understandability through pattern recognition."

6.2.4 Imagery and Photography Style

Imagery and photography are the nonverbal visual components of a communication system, encompassing photographic content, illustrations, iconography, and information graphics. These elements serve as powerful vehicles for emotional resonance, conceptual clarification, and brand recognition, working in concert with typography to form a complete visual language.

The adoption of a consistent visual style across all imagery is essential to brand integrity and user experience cohesion. This stylistic framework governs several key dimensions, including tonal quality (bright and airy versus dark and moody), authenticity (candid and documentary versus stylized and conceptual), color treatment (consistent palettes and grading), and subject matter focus. A well-defined style ensures that diverse visual elements are perceived as part of a cohesive whole, reinforcing brand identity across mediums and contexts. For instance, a hospital may employ authentic, warmly lit photographs to convey trust and compassion, while a technology company might use sleek, abstract illustrations to signal innovation and precision.

Iconography represents a specialized subsystem within visual imagery, serving as a symbolic shorthand for actions, concepts, and categories. Effective icon systems achieve visual coherence through consistent design parameters, including stroke weight, corner radius, level of detail, and stylistic approach (e.g., outlined, filled, or flat). This consistency reduces cognitive load by enabling users to quickly recognize and interpret symbols across different interfaces and applications. Beyond aesthetic uniformity, iconography must emphasize semantic clarity, ensuring that each symbol communicates its intended function unambiguously across cultural and contextual boundaries.

6.2.5 Layout and Composition

Layout and composition are the deliberate organization of all visual elements, including text, art, and space, within a given format, such as print, screen, or environmental design. This structural foundation shapes usability, navigability, and aesthetic impact by mediating the interaction between content and viewer through principles of visual perception and spatial logic.

The implementation of a grid system provides the basis for cohesive composition. Grids establish uniform alignments, proportionate ratios, and rhythmic spacing, transforming random placement into deliberate structure. Modular grids, hierarchical grids, and baseline grids each offer distinct advantages for various content types and media, ranging from multi-column journalistic layouts to single-screen application interfaces. By adhering to a grid, designers create consistent visual patterns that users instinctively internalize, enabling faster information processing and more intuitive interaction.

Complementary concepts enhance compositional effectiveness. The rule of thirds guides focal point placement through an invisible nine-part grid, recommending that key elements be positioned at intersection points to achieve dynamic equilibrium. Strategic use of white space (negative space) defines relationships between elements, creates visual breathing room, and isolates crucial content. White space is not merely empty area; it is an active design element that shapes perception and directs attention.

At the layout level, visual hierarchy organizes the user's path through content by distinguishing primary, secondary, and tertiary information. This is achieved through systematic variations in scale, contrast, placement, and spatial grouping. A successful layout presents information as a structured landscape with clear entry points, pathways, and destinations, enabling users to navigate complex material with ease. The ultimate goal is a composition that feels balanced and energetic, organized yet fluid, a visual environment in which form follows function to deliver experiences that are both aesthetically engaging and easily comprehensible.

6.3 Connecting Foundational Elements to Branding

A visual identity is the systematic transformation of abstract brand values into a specific visual language. This translation is achieved by deliberately applying core design principles, line, shape, space, value, color, and texture, to create the essential components of brand expression: logo, colour palette, typography, and imagery. Understanding this relationship is critical for developing unified, meaningful, and scalable brand systems.

These foundational elements serve as the building blocks from which all brand assets are derived. A logo, for example, is essentially a composition of lines and shapes arranged intelligently within positive and negative space. A colour palette represents the methodical application of color, guided by psychological principles and technical requirements. Typography is the artistic arrangement of lines and shapes into legible letterforms and logical hierarchies. The manipulation of value (through lighting and exposure), texture, and color establishes a consistent mood and tone, central to image style. This direct lineage assures that every brand manifestation from a business cards to digital interfaces, is built upon the same fundamental visual vocabulary, resulting in intrinsic harmony.

Each element carries certain semantic weight that directly shapes brand perception. The character of lines, whether sharp and geometric or organic and uneven, immediately communicates defining qualities. A technology company might employ crisp, straight lines to convey logic and efficiency, while an artisanal food business might favor hand-drawn, wavy lines to suggest authenticity and craftsmanship. This principle extends to custom typography and graphic styles, producing a cohesive formal language.

Shapes provide primordial, instantly recognizable forms that anchor brand meaning. Foundational shapes hold universal associations: circles and ovals symbolize community, unity, and tenderness, often appearing in social media icons or brands promoting inclusion; squares and rectangles represent stability, order, and trustworthiness, forming the basis of most card-based user interfaces and corporate identities; triangles convey direction, power, and dynamism, frequently used in warning signs, play buttons, and brands associated with science or innovation. A brand's consistent use of a dominant shape family communicates its essential message on a subconscious level, reinforcing identity through visual symbolism.

The strategic use of negative or white space is a hallmark of intelligent branding. Far from being empty, it functions as an active design element that defines relationships and conveys meaning. Clever applications of negative space, such as the hidden panda in the WWF emblem, create memorable and sophisticated brand marks. In user experience design, abundant and intentional white space is essential for reducing cognitive load, establishing clear information hierarchy, and cultivating an atmosphere of luxury, clarity, and focus.

Value, the spectrum of lightness and darkness, is fundamental to contrast, depth, and legibility. A brand's approach to value contrast shapes both its visual clarity and its mood. Apple, for example, employs high-value contrast to achieve maximum legibility and a crisp, modern aesthetic, while luxury fashion brands often favor low-contrast palettes with similar values to evoke subtlety, elegance, and refinement. Beyond aesthetics, value is critical for accessibility, as sufficient contrast between text and background is a non-negotiable requirement for inclusive design.

Color is the most psychologically powerful and emotionally charged design element. Its impact is governed by color theory, which must be applied with professional precision across media. A strong brand system carefully defines color in both additive models (RGB/HEX for screens) and subtractive models (CMYK/Pantone for print) to ensure complete consistency. The psychological associations of the chosen hues, such as blue for trust and green for growth, directly influence how audiences and experience a brand's personality.

Texture, whether expressed or implied, enhances depth, tactility, and individuality. The evolution of digital design styles, from the literal textures of skeuomorphism to the flat, textureless interfaces of the 2010s, and now to contemporary trends such as Neumorphism and Glassmorphism with their subtle shadows and blur effects, demonstrates texture's enduring role in creating sensory experience on a two-dimensional plane. The texture quality of a brand, whether smooth and glossy or rough and matte, communicates tangible characteristics and shapes emotional responses.

Design principles provide the framework for transforming these elements into a cohesive brand. They represent the "how" that governs the proper application of the "what." By deliberately varying value, color, or size, contrast heightens focus and intrigue. Balance arranges elements for visual stability, whether through symmetrical formality or asymmetrical dynamism. Emphasis establishes a clear focal point to direct primary attention. Movement guides the eye along a predetermined path through lines, shapes, or sequencing. Pattern and rhythm employ repetition to create unity and visual cadence. Finally, unity and harmony ensure that all individual elements and principles work together to form a single, compelling whole.

A powerful brand identity emerges through a purposeful synthesis process. Mastery of the primary elements provides the necessary visual vocabulary, while the disciplined application of design principles establishes the grammatical rules for combining them. Together, they create a visual identity system that transcends a mere collection of materials, becoming a coherent, expressive, and resonant language. This language conveys a brand's essence with clarity and emotion, gradually establishing familiarity and trust, and serving as the visual foundation for all user experiences and communications.

6.4 Conclusion

Visual design and branding function as the underlying languages through which objects express identity, purpose, and value. They extend beyond aesthetics to serve as cognitive frameworks that align interfaces with human perception through principles such as scale, hierarchy, balance, and contrast. This systematic approach manifests itself through the strategic construction of visual identity, where every element, from logos and psychologically calibrated color palettes to structured typography and coherent imagery, is grounded in the fundamental vocabulary of line, shape, space, value, color, and texture, ensuring consistent communication across all touchpoints. Visual coherence fosters trust by signalling professionalism and respect for the user, producing predictable patterns that reduce cognitive strain, accelerate interaction, and transform functional interfaces into intuitive experiences that feel both inevitable and essential in the digital landscape.

Chapter 7

Designing for All: The Interplay of Accessibility, Usability, and Inclusion

Creating digital experiences that are both intuitive and universally welcoming requires a holistic commitment to three interconnected principles: Usability, Accessibility, and Inclusion (AUI). Usability establishes the foundation by ensuring that users can achieve their objectives effectively, efficiently, and satisfactorily, while also addressing methods of evaluation and testing. The scope then expands to accessibility, demonstrating how to design for the full spectrum of human ability, from permanent disabilities to temporary or situational limitations, through adherence to standards such as WCAG. Inclusion represents the proactive practice of embracing human diversity in ability, language, and culture. By integrating these three principles (AUI), this chapter moves beyond mere compliance to illustrate how to design products that are not only functional but genuinely welcoming, meaningful, and effective for all users.

7.1 Defining the Core Concepts

To understand their synergy, each concept must be clearly defined. Together, they establish a hierarchy of focus: Usability asks whether a product functions effectively; Accessibility asks whether it works for people with impairments; and Inclusion asks whether everyone was considered from the outset.

DOI: 10.1201/9781003715764-7

7.1.1 Accessibility (A11y)

Accessibility (A11y) is the practice of designing and developing digital products, services, and environments so they can be used by people with disabilities. The shorthand "A11y" (where "11" represents the eleven letters between "A" and "y") has become standard terminology within the digital accessibility community. Accessibility focuses on removing barriers that might prevent individuals from interacting with or accessing digital products, addressing a wide range of disabilities, including:

- Visual impairments (such as blindness, low vision, or color blindness).
- Hearing impairments (such as deafness or partial hearing loss).
- Motor disabilities (such as limited fine motor control, tremors, or paralysis).
- Cognitive disabilities (such as learning difficulties, memory challenges, or attention disorders).
- Speech disabilities that affect verbal communication.

7.1.1.1 The Principles of Accessibility

The Web Content Accessibility Guidelines (WCAG) are organized around four fundamental principles, summarized by the acronym POUR. These principles establish a foundational framework for understanding the objectives of accessible design.

Perceivable

Perceivable information requires that all users must be able to recognize and comprehend the content and interface components presented to them, regardless of their sensory abilities. This principle ensures that information is never invisible to any sense. To achieve this, designers must provide text alternatives, commonly referred to as "alt text," for non-text content such as images, icons, and complex charts, enabling screen reader users to access meaning. Audio and video content must include captions and transcripts for individuals who are deaf or hard of hearing. Content should also be adaptable, capable of being presented in different layouts, such as single-column views or a high-contrast modes, without loss of information. Finally, content must remain distinguishable, which involves maintaining sufficient color contrast between text and background and allowing text resizing without disrupting the layout, thereby supporting users with low vision or color blindness.

Operable

Operable user interfaces ensure that all users can successfully interact with and navigate a system using methods that works for them. This principle extends beyond perception to guarantee that users can take meaningful action. A core requirement is full keyboard accessibility, allowing all every function to be reached and activated without a mouse, an essential feature for individuals with motor disabilities. Designers must also provide adequate time for users to read and complete tasks, avoiding timers that expire too quickly for those who need additional time to process information or physically engage with the interface. Equally important is the provision of safe content, which means avoiding flashing or blinking elements that exceed certain thresholds and could trigger seizures in individuals with photosensitive epilepsy. Finally, interfaces must be navigable, offering clear pathways to locate content and understand one's position within a site through mechanisms as logical heading structures, breadcrumbs, and descriptive links.

Understandable

Clear and predictable information and operations require that the user interface must be straightforward, enabling users to comprehend content and learn how to operate the system without confusion. This principle emphasizes cognitive accessibility. Text content should be readable and predictable, employing clear language and ensuring that interface behavior remains consistent with conventional patterns. Navigation and identification must also be uniform across the product; recurring elements such as menus and buttons should not change their location or behavior from page to page, as inconsistency can create significant barriers for users with cognitive disabilities. The system should further provide input assistance to help users avoid and correct mistakes, especially in forms, by offering clear and specific error messages and suggesting corrections whenever possible.

Robust

Robust content must be technically sound so it can be reliably interpreted by a wide range of current and future assistive technologies. This principle emphasizes the underlying technical quality of design and code, with the goal of maximizing compatibility with user agents and assistive tools such as screen readers, voice control software, and alternative input devices. Achieving robustness requires the use of valid, semantic HTML, meaning that elements are employed for their intended purpose, for example, using a $< button >$ element rather than a $< div >$ to represent a button. Semantic HTML communicates the structure, role, and state of interface components to assistive technologies, ensuring a dependable and consistent experience for all users as technology continues to evolve.

7.1.2 Usability

Usability is a multi-faceted concept defined through several key models. Jakob Nielsen (1994b) outlines a framework of five distinct attributes:

- Learnability: How easily users can accomplish basic tasks the first time they encounter the system.
- Efficiency: Measures the level of productivity achieved once users have become familiar with the system.
- Memorability: This considers how easily casual users can re-establish proficiency after a period of non-use.
- Errors: They address the system's ability to minimize errors, support easy recovery, and prevent catastrophic failures.
- Satisfaction: This evaluates how pleasant and enjoyable the system is to use.

Table 7.1: Comparison of usability attributes in ISO 9241-11 and Jacob Nielsen's framework.

Standard/ Framework	**Usability Attributes**	**Description**
ISO 9241-11	Effectiveness	Accuracy and completeness with which users achieve specified goals
	Efficiency	Resources expended in relation to the accuracy and completeness achieved
	Satisfaction	Freedom from discomfort and positive attitudes towards use
Jacob Nielsen	Learnability	How easy it is for users to accomplish basic tasks on first time they encounter a system
	Efficiency	How quickly users can perform tasks after learning the design
	Memorability	How easily users can re-establish proficiency after a period of non-use
	Errors/Safety	Number and severity of errors, and how easily users recover from them
	Satisfaction	How pleasant the design is to use

In contrast, the "ISO 9241-11" standard offers a more consolidated definition, describing usability as "the extent to which a product can be used by specified users to achieve specified goals with effectiveness, efficiency, and satisfaction in a specified context of use" (ISO 9241-11, 2018). This model is built on three core attributes:

- Effectiveness: The accuracy and completeness with which users achieve specified goals.
- Efficiency: The resources expended (e.g., time, effort) in relation to the goals achieved.
- Satisfaction: The degree to which users find the system comfortable and acceptable to use.

While the ISO standard does not explicitly list learnability, memorability, and errors as separate attributes, these qualities are often considered implicit within the three core components. For instance, a high error rate directly undermines efficiency, and poor learnability diminishes a new user's effectiveness (Van Welie et al., 1999). Table 7.2 illustrates the mapping of definitions between ISO 9241-11 and Nielsen, showing that both frameworks provide a concise outline of the concept of usability.

Table 7.2: Comparison of usability frameworks.

ISO 9241-11	**Jacob Nielsen**
Effectiveness	Memorability Errors/Safety
Efficiency	Efficiency Learnability
Satisfaction	Satisfaction

Example: A streamlined checkout process on an e-commerce site demonstrates high usability by enabling users to complete their purchase effectively (without errors), efficiently (with minimal time and steps), and satisfactorily (with confidence and a positive experience).

7.1.3 Inclusion

The overarching mindset and methodology of inclusion is the proactive practice of designing with diverse people, for the full range of human experience, to create solutions where everyone can belong and participate equally.

A core principle of inclusion is that it is proactive, not reactive. It actively seeks to identify and address potential points of exclusion during the initial planning and design phases. The goal is to prevent barriers from being created in the first place, rather than retrofitting solutions after the fact, which is often less effective and more costly.

This proactive approach is executed through a "with, not for" methodology. True inclusive design involves co-designing and collaborating directly with people from a wide range of backgrounds, particularly those from historically marginalized or excluded communities. It values their lived experiences as critical expertise, ensuring that the final product genuinely meets their needs.

The scope of inclusion is vast, encompassing permanent, temporary, and situational differences in ability, language, culture, gender, age, socioeconomic status, and neurodiversity. By acknowledging this spectrum, designers can create solutions that are resilient and useful for a much wider audience.

This often produces a powerful outcome known as the "curb-cut effect." When a solution is designed to meet the needs of one excluded group, such as sidewalk ramps for wheelchair users, it inevitably benefits many others, including parents with strollers or travelers with suitcases. Inclusive solutions, therefore, have a ripple effect of utility and convenience.

Ultimately, the central aim of inclusion is to rectify historical exclusion. It intentionally focuses on designing for groups that have been systematically overlooked or marginalized by traditional design processes. The primary goal is to create environments, products, and systems where everyone, without exception, has the opportunity to feel represented, valued, and able to participate fully.

7.2 Why This Trifecta is Non-Negotiable

As shown in Figure 7.1, the relationship among these principles is profoundly synergistic. The true strength of this framework lies in the interplay of its pillars whose impact is multiplicative, rather than merely additive. Focusing on one principle in isolation yields limited returns, as no single principle can be fully realized without the support of the others. A product can be technically accessible, meeting every guideline, yet remain frustrating and inefficient if it is not usable. Likewise, a product may be highly usable for a narrow, predefined audience but fail at inclusion by neglecting the needs of a diverse user base. When teams commit to all three principles in concert, the outcome transcends simple compliance. The result is a product that is robust, resilient, and thoughtfully crafted, delivering a superior experience that feels intuitive, welcoming, and empowering for a far broader spectrum of humanity.

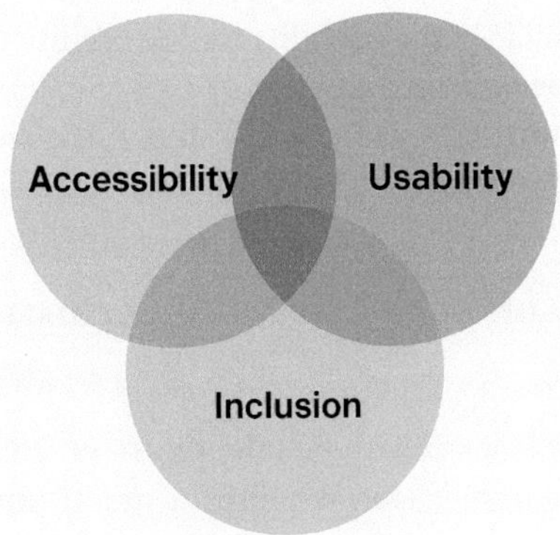

Figure 7.1: The interdependence of Accessibility, Usability, and Inclusion. The holistic user experience (center) is only achieved when all three principles are addressed in concert.

7.2.1 They are Deeply Interconnected and Overlapping

Good usability cannot exist without accessibility, and true inclusion cannot be achieved without both.

The "curb cut effect" offers a powerful real-world testament to the multiplicative strength of this trifecta. Originally designed as a solution for wheelchair users, the curb cut exemplifies Accessibility in the physical world. Yet its benefits quickly expanded, proving its inclusive design by serving parents with strollers, cyclists, travelers with rolling luggage, and delivery workers. This single intervention, aimed at one group, inadvertently made the urban landscape more usable for a vast and diverse population. By eliminating the need to navigate a steep ledge, it also fundamentally improved usability for everyone, creating a smoother, more efficient, and safer flow of pedestrian traffic. This demonstrates how a design decision rooted in accessibility, when viewed through an inclusive lens, inevitably produces a superior and more usable environment for all.

The development of closed captions provides a powerful digital parallel to the curb cut, perfectly illustrating the symbiotic relationship among these three principles. Originally engineered to ensure accessibility for Deaf and hard-of-hearing individuals, captions transcended their initial purpose to become a tool of profound inclusion. They now benefit a wide spectrum of users, from a student practicing a foreign language and a gym-goer in a noisy environment to a parent watching the news in a quiet household. By enabling content consumption in sound-sensitive or noisy contexts and aiding comprehension, captions significantly enhance the usability and flexibility of media for everyone. This evolution from a specialized accessibility tool to a universally valued feature underscores how designing for specific needs does not merely solve problems for a few, but innovates and improves the experience for the entire user base.

7.2.2 Ethical, Business and Legal Imperative

Ethical

Beyond the legal and business cases lies the profound ethical responsibility we bear as creators in the digital age. We have a moral duty to design products that do not exclude, marginalize, or create barriers for people. When we design primarily for an assumed default, the able-bodied, tech-savvy, English-speaking user, we consciously or unconsciously engage in digital discrimination, building a world where access to information, services, and community is unequal. This is not a passive oversight but an active choice that reinforces societal inequities. Ultimately, prioritizing accessibility, usability, and inclusion is an act of empathy and justice; it reflects a commitment to recognizing the inherent dignity and worth of every user. It is, quite simply, the right thing to do, and it represents the highest calling of our profession: to use our skills to build a more equitable and connected world for all.

Business

Excluding people through poor design is fundamentally bad for business, and the market shaped by accessibility and inclusion is far from a niche segment. With over one billion people worldwide living with a disability, and when considering their friends, family, and influencers, the economic power of this community often referred to as the "Purple Pound" or "Disability Dollar," is enormous and cannot be overlooked. Yet the business benefits extend far beyond this group. Inclusive design principles, such as clear language and simple navigation, enhance the experience for all users, leading to higher conversion rates, reduced bounce rates, and lower support costs. Moreover, features born from accessibility, like voice control and video captions, have evolved into mainstream expectations and significant market differentiators. Investing in this trifecta therefore not a charitable expense but a powerful competitive advantage, one that drives innovation, expands market share, and fosters deep, lasting brand loyalty.

Legal

From a legal standpoint, the stakes for neglecting digital accessibility have never been higher, as evidenced by a sharp rise in litigation and regulatory action worldwide. In the United States, websites are increasingly considered "places of public accommodation" under the Americans with Disabilities Act (ADA), leading to a flood of lawsuits against businesses with inaccessible online services. Similarly, Canada has enacted robust legislation such as the Accessibility for Ontarians with Disabilities Act (AODA), while the European Union is implementing the European Accessibility Act, which sets binding requirements for a wide range of digital products and services. This evolving legal landscape makes it clear that treating accessibility as an optional add-on is no longer just a design misstep; it is a direct and significant legal risk that can result in costly fines, mandatory redesigns, and substantial reputational damage. Consequently, a proactive commitment to accessibility is not merely about ethical design or market expansion, it is a fundamental requirement for legal compliance and corporate risk management in the digital age.

The economic case for this trifecta is equally compelling, beginning with the sheer scale of the market that accessible and inclusive design unlocks. With over one billion people worldwide living with a disability, this community represents a market the size of China that no business can rationally ignore. Yet the true reach extends far beyond this figure. When factoring in the friends, family, and colleagues influenced by their experiences, and who may choose brands that align with inclusive values, the addressable audience expands exponentially into a massive, global demographic. Inclusive design also inherently accommodates situational and temporary limitations, such as a person with a short-term injury, an aging population experiencing changing abilities, or a user navigating a challenging environment. By consciously designing to include this vast and diverse population, businesses are not simply checking an ethical box; they are making a strategic decision to tap into a multi-trillion-dollar market and drive significant growth.

The synergy between accessibility and Search Engine Optimization (SEO) is another powerful, yet often overlooked, business advantage. Many core accessibility practices align directly with the technical foundations that search engines reward. For instance, using a proper, logical heading structure (H1, H2, H3) not only helps screen reader users understand a page's organization but also provides a clear content hierarchy for search engine crawlers. Similarly, descriptive alt text for images serves the essential function of conveying meaning to users who are blind, while simultaneously supplying search engines with crucial context that allows those images to be indexed and appear in search results. Other practices, such as creating descriptive link text, providing transcripts for audio content, and ensuring a fast, mobile-friendly experience, enhance both accessibility and search rankings. Therefore, investing in accessibility is not just about human users; it is also about optimizing for your most important robotic user, the search engine crawler, making it a fundamental component of any successful digital marketing strategy.

In today's competitive marketplace, authentic gestures of inclusion have become a powerful differentiator that directly drive brand loyalty. When users see themselves reflected in a company's products and services, whether through accessible features, inclusive imagery, or considerate design, they feel recognized, valued, and respected. This emotional connection transcends simple customer satisfaction; it fosters a deeper, trust-based relationship. For individuals who are often excluded by mainstream design, discovering a brand that thoughtfully accommodates their needs can inspire relief and appreciation that translates into fierce, long-term allegiance. These users do not merely become customers; they evolve into brand advocates who enthusiastically recommend the company within their communities. Such loyalty is difficult for competitors to replicate, as it is built on a foundation of demonstrated empathy and a genuine commitment to "doing the right thing," ultimately transforming the brand into a symbol of inclusivity and respect.

7.2.3 Inclusion is the Proactive Mindset that Unlocks the other Two

Treating accessibility as a mere checklist to be verified at the end of a project is a fundamentally flawed and inefficient approach. This retroactive tactic often produces a clunky, "bolted-on" experience in which features like screen reader compatibility or keyboard navigation feel like afterthoughts rather than integral parts of the design. Such solutions are typically more costly and time-consuming to implement and frequently create a subpar, disjointed user experience. This is precisely why the philosophy of Inclusion is so vital; it serves as the proactive antidote to this problem. By embedding inclusive thinking from the very beginning, during research, ideation, and wireframing, we naturally design with a broader range of human needs in mind. This shift-left approach ensures that accessibility considerations are woven into the fabric of the product, yielding solutions that are not only compliant but also seamless, intuitive, and inherently superior for everyone.

Beginning the design process with an inclusive mindset fundamentally changes the foundational questions we ask. Instead of the narrow query, "Does this work for our target user?", we are compelled to ask the more expansive and empathetic question: "Who might be left out by this design decision?" This single, proactive inquiry acts as a powerful catalyst, guiding teams to consider accessibility from the earliest stages of research, ideation, and prototyping. Shifting accessibility left is not only a more dignified approach but a profoundly practical one: it identifies potential barriers when they are easiest and least expensive to fix, saving significant time, resources, and costly rework later in the development cycle. By designing to include those at the margins, we are compelled to innovate and create flexible, robust solutions that inherently accommodate a wider range of human ability and context. The result is not merely a product accessible to some, but one that is more resilient, adaptable, and usable for all.

An authentically inclusive design process actively engages a diverse spectrum of users throughout research and testing, serving as the most effective way to uncover real-world barriers that a homogeneous design team, no matter how skilled or empathetic, might never anticipate. When a team lacks diversity in ability, age, culture, and background, it operates with a collective blind spot, designing based on its own shared experiences and assumptions. By contrast, involving users who navigate the world differently, such as someone who relies on a screen reader, a person with low literacy, or an individual for whom English is a second language, reveals unforeseen challenges and nuances. This direct engagement transforms abstract principles into tangible insights, exposing issues ranging from confusing iconography and complex language to incompatible assistive technologies and culturally insensitive content. In practice, inclusion shifts from a theoretical aspiration to an evidence-based process, ensuring the final product is not merely built for a diverse audience but with them, resulting in solutions genuinely informed by the realities of human experience.

7.2.4 The Consequences of Ignoring the Trifecta

Accessible but not Usable

A significant pitfall in design occurs when a product is "accessible but not usable." This describes a situation in which a website or application may technically meet accessibility checkpoints, such as those outlined in WCAG, yet its overall design is so convoluted, illogical, or frustrating that it remains ineffective for everyone. Imagine a site with perfect color contrast and full keyboard navigation but a confusing menu structure, inconsistent labeling, and a laborious, multi-step process for simple tasks. In this scenario, a screen reader user can technically access all the content, but only by navigating a labyrinth of poor information architecture. Simultaneously, a user without a disability would likely abandon the site out of sheer frustration. This illustrates that technical compliance is merely the foundation; without thoughtful, user-centered design principles, accessibility alone cannot deliver a successful or positive user experience. It may fulfill the letter of the law but entirely misses its spirit.

Usable but not Accessible

A beautiful, intuitive app that cannot be used by a blind person with a screen reader is a profoundly flawed product, despite its surface-level appeal. This scenario exemplifies a critical failure in "usable but not accessible" design, where the experience is polished for a narrow segment of users while entirely excluding others. An app may feature sleek animations and a seamless gesture-based interface for sighted users, but if its underlying code lacks proper labels, semantic structure, and alternative text, it becomes a digital prison for those relying on a screen readers. This exclusion is not a minor oversight; it is a fundamental flaw that discriminates against a significant portion of the population, violating both ethical design principles and legal standards. It exposes the superficiality of the app's intuitiveness which was built on the assumption that all users perceive and interact with the world in the same way. Ultimately, a product that is not accessible to all cannot be truly considered well-designed, as good design is, by definition, inclusive and equitable.

Neither Accessible nor Usable, and Built without Inclusion

This combination, a product that is neither accessible nor usable, built without an inclusive mindset, represents the worst-case scenario in design. Such a product is broken on multiple levels: it alienates and excludes people with disabilities while simultaneously frustrating and inefficient for the general user. Born from a narrow, homogenous perspective that failed to ask "Who are we leaving out?", it is fundamentally ill-equipped for the modern, global market. It disregards the legal risks of inaccessibility, forfeits the vast economic potential of inclusive design, and fails the basic ethical test of equity. In today's competitive landscape, this lack of foresight and empathy becomes a critical vulnerability, producing a product that destined to be perceived as outdated, careless, and inferior, ultimately failing both commercially and culturally.

7.3 Essential Tools and Techniques

Understanding the philosophical "why" and the conceptual "what" of accessible design is a critical foundation, but it represents only half the challenge for practitioners. To move from theory to tangible results, one must also master the practical "how." This section serves as a hands-on toolkit, offering a comprehensive overview of essential software, established standards, and proven methods for implementing, testing, and validating accessibility and inclusion at every stage of the product development lifecycle. It bridges the gap between intention and execution, equipping designers, developers, and product managers with the concrete resources needed to build digital experiences that are truly for everyone.

7.3.1 Foundational Standards and Guidelines (The Rulebook)

Before any tool can be used effectively, one must first understand the benchmarks against which success is measured. Foundational standards and guidelines serve as this essential rulebook, providing the objective criteria that inform every design and development decision. At the core of this foundation are the Web Content Accessibility Guidelines (WCAG), an internationally recognized standard developed by the World Wide Web Consortium (W3C)[1]. As noted above, WCAG is structured around the four principles of POUR, ensuring that content is Perceivable, Operable, Understandable, and Robust. In practice, teams should aim for Level AA conformance as the baseline, since this level addresses the most significant and common barriers without the imposing the extensive demands of some AAA criteria. While accessibility should move beyond a mere box-ticking exercise, the specific success criteria within WCAG remain the definitive checklist for both manual and automated testing, providing clear technical requirements such as the minimum color contrast ratios defined in guideline 1.4.3.

For more complex, dynamic web applications, another W3C specification, WAI-ARIA (Accessible Rich Internet Applications)[2], becomes indispensable. ARIA provides a framework for making advanced widgets, live content updates, and single-page applications accessible to assistive technologies by supplementing HTML. Its strength lies in three core features: “roles” to define what an element is (e.g., role=“navigation”), “properties” to provide additional information (e.g., aria-required=“true”), and “states” to describe current conditions (e.g., aria-expanded=“false”). However, a key principle when using ARIA is to treat it as a repair tool rather than a primary solution. Developers should always prefer native HTML elements like < *button* > or < *nav* > whenever possible, since they come with built-in accessibility semantics and keyboard behavior. ARIA should be reserved to fill gaps only when native elements are insufficient for the intended interaction.

7.3.2 Design and Prototyping Tools (Building it Right from the Start)

Integrating accessibility considerations during the design and prototyping phase is one of the most effective ways to prevent costly and time-consuming rework during development. A primary method for achieving this is through the use of accessibility plugins integrated directly into design software. Tools such as the Stark suite for Figma, Sketch, and Adobe XD embed accessibility checks into the designer’s workflow as shown in Figure 7.2. These plugins provide several critical capabilities: a color contrast checker that instantly validates palettes against WCAG standards; vision simulation modes that allow designers to view their creations through the lens of various forms of color blindness; the ability to annotate focus order for interactive elements; and tools to verify that layouts

[1] `https://www.w3.org/TR/WCAG21/`

[2] `https://www.w3.org/WAI/standards-guidelines/aria/`

remain functional and legible when text is scaled to 200%, ensuring designs are robust for users with low vision.

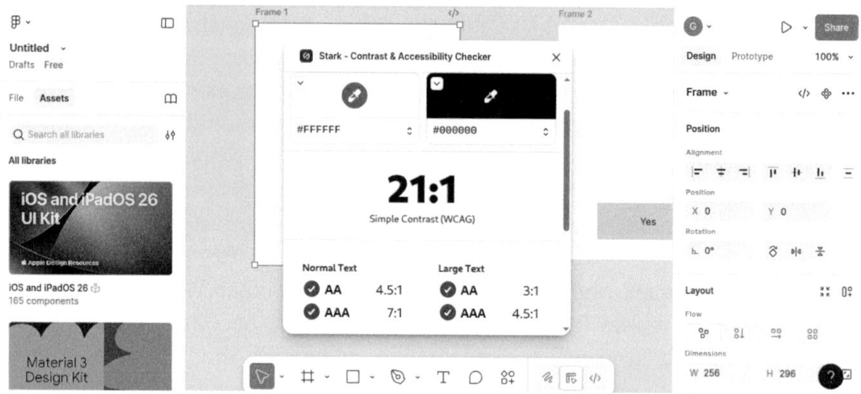

Figure 7.2: Accessibility plugins like stark tool for Figma.

Beyond individual plugins, a more systematic and scalable approach is accessible design system management. This practice involves formally documenting accessibility requirements directly within the component library used by the entire product team. For example, the documentation for a Button component would specify not only its visual appearance but also its minimum contrast ratios for all states (default, hover, disabled), the required style for its focus indicator, any ARIA attributes developers should implement for dynamic states (such as aria-live for a loading button), and the expected keyboard and screen reader behavior. By embedding these specifications directly into the foundational building blocks of the product's design language, teams establish consistency, efficiency, and a stronger baseline of accessibility from the very beginning of the development process.

7.3.3 Development and Testing Tools (Building it Right and Checking Your Work)

Once a design moves into development, a new set of tools and techniques is required to ensure the finished product aligns with its accessible intent. Automated accessibility testing tools serve as a crucial first line of defense, scanning code or live webpages to quickly identify a range of common technical issues. The engine known as axe-core is widely regarded as the gold standard in this space and can be integrated in multiple ways; its browser extension enables manual checks during development, while its integration into Continuous Integration/Continuous Deployment (CI/CD) pipelines via tools like axe-linter can automatically fail a build if new critical errors are introduced, effectively "shifting left" and embedding accountability into the engineering process. Another invaluable tool is the WAVE browser extension from WebAIM, which provides a visual, in-context representation of a page's accessibility structure by highlighting headings, landmarks, and form labels, while also flagging errors in an intuitive overlay format.

Manual testing is essential because automatic technologies can detect 30–40% of accessibility issues. The most fundamental of these is keyboard-only navigation, which entails unplugging the mouse and navigating solely with the Tab, Shift+Tab, Enter, and arrow keys. This basic test reveals critical usability concerns by assessing whether all interactive information is accessible, whether the focus indicator is consistently visible and clear, and whether the tab order is logical. Screen reader testing is equally vital, requiring familiarity with the fundamentals of a primary screen readers, such as NVDA with Firefox on Windows or VoiceOver with Safari on macOS.

Such testing ensures that content is announced in a logical order, form fields are properly labeled, button functions are evident even without visual context, and complicated widgets accurately announce their state. For larger organizations, establishing dedicated Assistive Technology (AT) Testing Bays with diverse configurations of operating systems, browsers, and assistive technologies, such as JAWS, Dragon NaturallySpeaking, and ZoomText, helps ensures testing is consistent, comprehensive, and reproducible across platforms.

7.3.4 User-Centered Validation Techniques (The Ultimate Test)

While tools and checklists are useful, the most important and informative strategies entail bringing in real users, who provide the ultimate validation of a product's accessibility and inclusion. Inclusive Usability Testing entails recruiting volunteers with a variety of disabilities, including visual, auditory, motor, and cognitive impairments, and observing them as they attempt to complete realistic tasks with the product.

The logistics of this testing are critical; recruitment often requires collaboration with disability advocacy organizations or specialized agencies; participants must be fairly compensated for their time and expertise; and the testing environment, whether in person or remote, must be comfortable and accessible, including the platform used for remote sessions. This process delivers unmatched results, uncovering real-world usability issues and subtle challenges that automated tools and heuristic evaluations cannot detect. Most importantly, it provides the empathy and deep insight required to build experiences that are genuinely inclusive.

In addition to user testing, a formal Accessibility Audit and Expert Review conducted by a certified accessibility professional provides a thorough, rigorous examination of a product's compliance and usability. To produce a comprehensive report, the expert employs a combination of methodologies, including automated tools, rigorous manual tests with various assistive technologies, and cross-checking against the entire WCAG checklist. The resulting report not only identifies infractions but also explains their impact on users and offers precise, prioritized recommendations for remediation. This type of audit is frequently used as a final compliance check before a major launch or as a baseline for developing a new, organization-wide accessibility strategy.

It is important to recognize that no single technology or technique can serve as a panacea for attaining digital accessibility. A mature and effective accessibility practice is deliberate and multifaceted, incorporating multiple strategies to maximize coverage and understanding. Automated tools are used for their efficiency and scalability across large codebases, uses manual testing assesses the usability of complex interactions and nuanced design patterns, and user-centred validation grounds the work in real human experience and empathy. By thoughtfully integrating this entire toolbox into every team's standard workflow, from design to development to QA, an organization can move beyond theorizing about inclusion to actively and consistently embedding it into the fabric of its digital products.

Table 7.3: The AUI practitioner's toolkit.

Phase	Key Standards/Tools	Primary Technique
Planning & Guidelines	WCAG, WAI-ARIA	Define conformance target (AA), use semantic HTML first.
Design & Prototyping	Stark, Contrast Checkers, Design Systems	Annotate focus order, simulate impairments, document specs.
Development & Testing	axe-core, WAVE, Keyboard, Screen Readers (NVDA/VoiceOver)	Automated CI checks, manual keyboard/screen reader testing.
Validation	Inclusive Usability Testing, Expert Audit	Recruit diverse users, conduct expert review against WCAG.

7.4 Conclusion: A Responsibility and an Opportunity

Designing for Accessibility, Usability, and Inclusion (AUI) goes beyond technical compliance; it represents a fundamental shift in mindset. It challenges us to reject the notion of a 'typical user' and instead engage with the rich diversity of human experience. This paradigm acts as a powerful catalyst for creativity, encouraging deeper empathy, critical reflection, and the development of more resilient, ethical, and successful solutions. The tools and approaches presented here provide a clear path forward. Embracing the AUI mindset is no longer a niche speciality, it is a core competency and a professional imperative. It is our shared responsibility and greatest opportunity to create a digital world that truly includes everyone.

References

Aguayo Publicidad. (2018). *Zeigarnik effect: How to apply it in ux.* https://aguayo.co/en/blog-aguayp-user-experience/zeigarnik-effect-how-to-apply-it-in-ux/#:~:text=The%20Zeigarnik%20Effect%20highlights%20the,and%20engaging%20experiences%20for%20users. (Accessed: July 6, 2024)

Babich N. (2022). *Information architecture design: A step-by-step guide.* https://uxplanet.org/information-architecture-design-a-step-by-step-guide-41dcd4405ee3. (Accessed: September 25, 2025)

Benjamin Ball. (2024). *How to use the rule of three in communication.* https://benjaminball.com/blog/how-to-use-the-rule-of-three/. (Accessed: September 2, 2025)

Brown, D. (2010). Eight principles of information architecture. *Bulletin of the American Society for Information Science and Technology*, *36*(6), 30–34.

Dickerson, J. (2013). *Walt disney: The world's first ux designer.* https://uxmag.com/articles/walt-disney-the-worlds-first-ux-designer. (Accessed: November 9, 2025)

Disha Mod. (2024). *Von restorff effect: Ux law of distinctiveness.* https://blog.uxtweak.com/von-restorff-effect/#:~:text=The%20Von%20Restorff%20effect%2C%20or,be%20remembered%20than%20other%20items. (Accessed: July 6, 2024)

Dreyfuss, H. (1959). Designing for people. *Design*, *61*(2), 80–83.

EMILY STEVENS. (2021). *The fascinating history of ux design: A definitive timeline.* https://careerfoundry.com/en/blog/ux-design/the

-fascinating-history-of-ux-design-a-definitive-timeline/. (Accessed: July 3, 2024)

Fathima. (2023). *5 steps of the ui/ux design process every expert follows.* https://www.aufaitux.com/blog/ui-ux-design-process/#:~:text=An%20effective%20UI%2FUX%20design,user%20requirements%20and%20business%20goals. (Accessed: July 1, 2024)

Fitzgerald, A. (2023). *What is hick's law & why does it matter for ux.* https://blog.hubspot.com/website/information-overload. (Accessed: July 6, 2024)

Garrett, J. (2002). *The elements of user experience: User-centered design for the web.* New Riders. Retrieved from https://books.google.co.in/books?id=6bPTRJ7xkFkC

Gibbons, S. (2018). *Empathy mapping: The first step in design thinking.* https://www.nngroup.com/articles/empathy-mapping/. (Accessed: September 7, 2025)

Gordon, K.. (2020). *5 principles of visual design in ux.* https://www.nngroup.com/articles/principles-visual-design/. (Accessed: October 10, 2025)

Gordon, K. (2022). *Using grids in interface designs.* https://www.nngroup.com/articles/using-grids-in-interface-designs/. (Accessed: December 22, 2025)

Holla, M. (2018). *The eight principles of information architecture.* https://medium.com/@mattholla/the-eight-principles-of-information-architecture-6feff11f907a. (Accessed: July 14, 2024)

Hugo Raymond. (2024). *What is the difference between ui and ux?* https://www.figma.com/resource-library/difference-between-ui-and-ux/. (Accessed: June 30, 2024)

Interaction Design Foundation - IxDF. (2016). *What are the gestalt principles?. interaction design foundation - ixdf.* https://www.interaction-design.org/literature/topics/gestalt-principles. (Accessed: July 06, 2024)

Interaction Design Foundation - IxDF. (2021). *What is human-centered design (hcd).* https://www.interaction-design.org/literature/topics/human-centered-design. (Accessed: July 07, 2024)

ISO 9241-11. (2018). *Ergonomics of human-system interaction part 11: Usability: Definitions and concepts.* https://www.iso.org/standard/63500.html. (Accessed: October 28, 2025)

Kahn, P., & Lenk, K. (1998). Design: principles of typography for user interface design. *interactions*, *5*(6), 15.

Lischer, B. (2024). *Ignyte branding agency.* https://www.ignytebrands.com/the-psychology-of-color-in-branding/. (Accessed: December 22, 2025)

Mads Soegaard. (2023). *Ux vs ui: What's the difference?* https://www.interaction-design.org/literature/article/ux-vs-ui-what-s-the-difference. (Accessed: June 30, 2024)

Mann, N. (2023). *How to create a customer journey map: A step-by-step breakdown.* https://www.woopra.com/blog/customer-journey-map. (Accessed: September 7, 2025)

McCay, A. (2024). *Creating a persona—a step-by-step guide with tips and examples.* https://uxpressia.com/blog/how-to-create-persona-guide-examples. (Accessed: September 7, 2025)

Morville, P., & Rosenfeld, L. (2006). *Information architecture for the world wide web: Designing large-scale web sites.* " O'Reilly Media, Inc.".

Nielsen, J. (1994a). 10 usability heuristics for user interface design. *Nielsen Norman Group.* Retrieved from https://www.nngroup.com/articles/ten-usability-heuristics/ (Updated January 30, 2024)

Nielsen, J. (1994b). *Usability engineering.* Morgan Kaufmann.

Nielsen, J. (2023). *Jakob's law of the internet user experience.* https://www.uxtigers.com/post/jakobs-law. (Accessed: July 6, 2024)

Norman, D. (1988). *The psychology of everyday things.* Basic Books.

Norman, D. (1990). *The design of everyday things* (No. no. 842). Doubleday. Retrieved from https://books.google.co.in/books?id=b09jQgAACAAJ

Norman Donald, A. (2013). *The design of everyday things.* MIT Press.

Raluca Budiu. (2022). *Fitts's law and its applications in ux.* https://www.nngroup.com/articles/fitts-law/. (Accessed: July 6, 2024)

Resmini, A., & Rosati, L. (2012). A brief history of information architecture. *Journal of information architecture*, *3*(2), 33–45.

Richard Greenan. (2023). *What is miller's law in ux design? a complete guide.* https://careerfoundry.com/en/blog/ux-design/what-is-millers-law/. (Accessed: July 6, 2024)

Ripalda, D., Guevara, C., & Garrido, A. (2020). Framework based on gestalt principles to design mobile interfaces for a better user experience. In *International conference on applied human factors and ergonomics* (pp. 158–165).

Rosenfeld, L., Morville, P., & Arango, J. (2015). *Information architecture: for the web and beyond.* " O'Reilly Media, Inc.".

Shashi Shekhar Shukla. (2023). *Importance of ui/ux design in creating digital products.* https://bootcamp.uxdesign.cc/importance-of-ui-ux-design-in-creating-digital-products-c3eee5238587. (Accessed: June 30, 2024)

Sonowal, G. (2025). *Design thinking: Innovative solutions for a better world.* CRC Press.

Spencer, D. (2010). *A practical guide to information architecture* (Vol. 1). Five Simple Steps Penarth.

Stevens, E. (2023). *Guide to 7 types of logo design with examples.* https://www.andacademy.com/resources/blog/graphic-design/types-of-logo-design/. (Accessed: October 12, 2025)

Taylor, F. (1911). *The principles of scientific management.* Harper.

Uddin, N. (2023). *A brief history and evolution of ui ux design.* https://musemind.agency/blog/ui-ux-design-history#:~:text=With%20the%20rise%20of%20the,practice%20began%20to%20take%20shape. (Accessed: July 3, 2024)

uxplanet.org. (2024). *Information architecture design step-by-step.* https://uxplanet.org/information-architecture-design-step-by-step-7036897511d7. (Accessed: September 25, 2025)

Van Welie, M., Van Der Veer, G. C., & Eliëns, A. (1999). Breaking down usability. In *Interact* (pp. 613–620).

Wojtynek, L., Kulińska, E., Dendera-Gruszka, M., & Kulińska, K. (2018). Implementation of lean 5s methodology in logistic enterprise. *Research in Logistics & Production*, *8*, 179–187.

Wurman, R. (1989). *Information anxiety* (No. v. 1). Doubleday. Retrieved from https://books.google.co.in/books?id=f8ZoAAAAIAAJ

Index

D

E

F

G

H

I

J

K

L

M

N

O

P

R